CULTURE SHOCK!

Sweden

Charlotte Rosen Svensson

Graphic Arts Center Publishing Company
Portland, Oregon

In the same series

Argentina	Ecuador	Laos	Sri Lanka
Australia	Egypt	Malaysia	Sweden
Austria	Finland	Mauritius	Switzerland
Belgium	France	Mexico	Syria
Bolivia	Germany	Morocco	Taiwan
Borneo	Greece	Myanmar	Thailand
Brazil	Hong Kong	Nepal	Turkey
Britain	Hungary	Netherlands	UAE
California	India	Norway	Ukraine
Canada	Indonesia	Pakistan	USA
Chile	Iran	Philippines	USA—The South
China	Ireland	Saudi Arabia	Venezuela
Costa Rica	Israel	Scotland	Vietnam
Cuba	Italy	Singapore	
Czech Republic	Japan	South Africa	
Denmark	Korea	Spain	

Barcelona At Your Door	Paris At Your Door	A Student's Guide
Beijing At Your Door	Rome At Your Door	A Traveller's Medical
Chicago At Your Door	San Francisco At Your	Guide
Havana At Your Door	Door	A Wife's Guide
Jakarta At Your Door	Shanghai At Your Door	Living and Working
Kuala Lumpur, Malaysia	Tokyo At Your Door	Abroad
At Your Door	Vancouver At Your Door	Personal Protection At
London At Your Door		Home & Abroad
Moscow At Your Door	A Globe-Trotter's Guide	Working Holidays
Munich At Your Door	A Parent's Guide	Abroad
New York At Your Door		

Illustrations by TRIGG

© 1996 Times Editions Pte Ltd
© 2000 Times Media Private Limited
Revised 2000, 2003
Reprinted 1997, 1998, 1999, 2001, 2003

This book is published by special
arrangement with Times Media Private Limited
Times Centre, 1 New Industrial Road, Singapore 536196
International Standard Book Number 1-55868-760-2
Library of Congress Catalog Number 96-77212
Graphic Arts Center Publishing Company
P.O. Box 10306 • Portland, Oregon 97296-0306 • (503) 226-2402

Printed in Singapore

CONTENTS

ACKNOWLEDGEMENTS

My sincere thanks to Monica Rabe for letting me use her book *Living and Working in Sweden* (published by Tre Böcker Förlag AB, Göteborg, Sweden in 1994) as a source of reference when writing *Culture Shock! Sweden.*

Living and Working in Sweden has been of invaluable help to me, in particular when writing the following chapters:

- From Vikings to the Swedish Model
- The Swedish People
- Business in Sweden

For specific help with this book, I would like to thank Robert Grahm, who contibuted beautiful photographs at very short notice. Britt and Dennis Eliasson, Malin Eliasson and Bengt Johansson, and Anette Nilsson and Peder Bengtsson kindly let me have photographs directly out of their own albums, for which I am very grateful.

Both Elly and Roland Svensson helped immensely with telephone advice, fact-checking, and conversations about Swedish customs and culture, while Patrick Schyum offered advice and help on the various food sections, and with talking about Swedish customs in general.

Thanks also to my parents and to Catherine Neil for constant encouragement, and to Bengt, for reading and commenting on the manuscript, as well as being the 'in-house expert' – it would have been impossible without his help.

When I moved to Sweden I was often daunted by the differences I encountered – and this after living in several different countries! Many of my Swedish partner's friends made me feel very welcome and introduced me to a Sweden I grew slowly to enjoy and appreciate greatly. Especial thanks for this to Annika and Göran Johansson, Erika Biesse and Lars Wessman and Kate Parr-Grahm and Robert Grahm.

Finally, many Swedish and non-Swedish friends helped with countless discussions of culture, and with sending me articles about anything conceivably of interest for the book. All of this assistance and support has been greatly appreciated.

SWEDEN

NORWEGIAN

SEA

Arctic Circle

Mount Kebnekaise
(6,945 ft./2,116 m)

Kiruna

Mount
Sarekhåkkå

Jokkmokk

N

NORR-
BOTTEN

LAPPLAND

VÄSTER-
BOTTEN

Umeå

Gulf of

JÄMTLAND

ÅNGER-
MANLAND

N o r r l a n d

FINLAND

HÄRJEDALEN

MEDELPAD

HÄLSING-
LAND

NORWAY

Kölen Range

S v e a l a n d

DALARNA

GÄSTRIK-
LAND

UPPLAND

VÄSTMANLAND

Uppsala

VÄRMLAND

STOCKHOLM

DALS-
LAND

NÄRKE

SÖDERMANLAND

ESTONIA

ÖSTER-

BOHUSLÄN

VÄSTER-
GÖTLAND

GÖTLAND

Gotland

Göteborg

G ö t a l a n d

GOTLAND

BALTIC SEA

HALLAND

SMÅLAND

Kalmar

ÖLAND

LATVIA

Öland

DENMARK

SKÅNE

BLEKINGE

Malmö

LITHUANIA

POLAND

*Sweden occupies the eastern and largest sector of the Scandinavian Peninsula.
Its northernmost region, Norrland, lies partly within the Arctic Circle.*

Chapter One

INTRODUCING SWEDEN

A book about Sweden – it ought to be easy to categorise the ups and downs of Swedish living, culture, language and people. After all, it is a very small country with only 8.9 million people, and is one of the most homogeneous populations in the world. Swedes are tall, blonde and blue-eyed, and their country is very cold and snowy, with polar bears and reindeer. Everyone skis and plays ice hockey, and is a pacifist, not liking confrontation. Of course it is one of the sexiest nations on earth, as everyone knows from tales of Swedish models and au pairs, and morals are a little looser. Other facts about Sweden that 'everyone' knows are how expensive everything is there, how left wing Swedish politics are, that Sweden welcomes political refugees and contributes greatly to international aid, that Swedish food is not up to much and that Swedish culture is a mix of very depressing, deep hidden meaning type films à la Bergman and light bouncy pop music like Abba's and The Cardigans'.

But the reality, as always, is different. Describing and learning about Sweden is much more complicated than the image of blondes from a cold country would imply! In this book you will find lots of information on the myths and realities of Swedish people, politics, geography, culture and everyday living. I hope that it will be helpful to anyone planning to move to or travel within Sweden, or to anyone who just needs to know more about the country.

You will learn about the dark-haired, dark-eyed Swedes, the indigenous Saami people and the many immigrants who have settled in Sweden. You will read about the long sunny beaches in the south, the rocky coastline on the west coast and the great forests and long winters in the country's north. No, there are no polar bears anywhere in Sweden, but the wildlife is varied and there are still large areas of unspoiled habitat and wilderness in Sweden, unlike most of the rest of Europe.

Not everyone skis – football is very popular and Sweden came third in the 1994 World Football Championships. Swedes surf, golf, swim, run and, of course, play tennis. In fact they enjoy the same sports as most other Western nations and excel in many of them. It is true that Swedes are proud of their neutral status and most avoid confrontation. However, they are also proud of their bloodthirsty warrior history and of the Viking times, and volunteer for United Nations armed forces around the world. Many Swedes are sexy. Many Swedes are not. Some have looser morals and some very strict, although it is true that certain behaviour considered immoral in other countries, such as living together without being married, and divorce, is acceptable in Sweden.

And so on – there is much which is homogenous in Sweden compared with, for example, the United States, but there is still a wealth of diversity which is what makes Sweden such a fascinating place to visit and a very pleasant place to live.

THE REGIONS OF SWEDEN

Traditionally, Sweden is divided into three regions. The northern half of the country, Norrland, is very sparsely populated with a mixture of Swedes and Sámi, the native nomadic peoples who migrate throughout northern Scandinavia. The southern quarter, called Götaland because of the Götes who lived there and the middle quarter, called Svealand because of the Sveas who lived there, have a mixture of densely populated cities and sparsely populated countryside, and a mixture too of Swedes and immigrants. In fact, the name *Sverige* (Sweden in Swedish) is taken from 'The Kingdom of the Sveas' – *Svea-rike*. Rike, of course, means kingdom. In modern Swedish this developed into Sverige.

Norrland

Norrland is the biggest part of Sweden, but few Swedes live there. The winters are very long and the summers short. In fact, the official first day of summer is not until the middle of June while the last day is in the middle of August. Summer in Sweden is defined as a time when the average temperature is above 10°C (50°F). In the very far north, around Kiruna, the sun does not set for a month in the summer and does not rise for a month in the winter.

Norrland is also one of the last true wilderness areas in Europe, with two of the largest national parks, Abisko and Sarek, protected from development. Norrland features Sweden's highest mountain, Kebnekaise, which stands 2,111 metres (6,930 feet) tall and is part of the 1,000 kilometre long and 100 kilometre wide mountain range to the west which forms a natural border with Norway. Norway is also the neighbouring country to the north, while the Tårne River runs along the border with Finland. Sweden has no other borders as it is surrounded by the Baltic Sea and the North Sea on its eastern, southern and southwestern sides.

Just a small part of Sweden is north of the Arctic Circle, but even there the weather is mild during the summer because of the warming

The open expanses of northern Sweden are part of Europe's last wilderness.

properties of the Gulf Stream. In the winter, northernmost Lappland (a part of Norrland) has more than 220 days of snow. As can be imagined, the farmers work short intensive seasons! Most of the best Swedish ski resorts are in Jämtland in southern Norrland, including Storlien, Duved and Åre, where World Cup skiing events are held.

Svealand

Svealand is the heart of Sweden, including Stockholm, Uppsala and Värmland. Stockholm, with over a million people, is like a big city anywhere, with its fast-paced city life and accompanying pleasures and frustrations. However, Värmland typifies rural Swedish life, with red farmhouses, forests and lakes. Many of the biggest lakes in Sweden, and parts of the very largest, Vänern and Vättern, are in Svealand, as are some of the more popular ski resorts such as Sälen and Idre. The mountains aren't as high as in Norrland, but they are still beautiful and much more accessible.

Götaland

The southern part of Sweden was originally Denmark in Viking times, and there are still some accents and customs which are similar to Danish ones. The landscape tends to be flatter and warmer, with small lakes and hills instead of the great rivers and mountains of the north. The second and third largest cities in Sweden, Gothenburg *(Göteborg* in Swedish) and Malmö, are in the south. So too are the large glass blowing region called Glasriket in Småland and the popular holiday islands of Gotland and Öland to the east. Although the way of living in Götaland is similar to that in northern Germany and Denmark, there are still expanses of unoccupied and uninhabited land because the population is so unevenly distributed. Over 22% of the population of Sweden lives in just three cities, and most of the rest live in smaller cities such as the university towns of Uppsala in Svealand and Lund in the south (near Malmö).

Breaking the country up into three regions is the traditional Swedish division. However, there are two more ways of dividing up the country – into counties *(län)* and into municipalities *(kommuner)*. Often Swedes will speak of coming from a specific county rather than from a city or an area, defining themselves, for example, as coming from Halland (on the southwest coast) or from Dalarna.

CLIMATE

Naturally, Sweden's climate varies greatly from north to south, but overall it is a temperate and cool climate. The coldest month of the year is January in the north and February in the south, and the warmest is July everywhere. The length of days is much shorter in winter and much longer in summer in Sweden than in most other countries because it is so far north, and that affects the temperature greatly as well. Another climatic difference is that the east coast tends to be drier and sunnier, while the west coast is wetter and windier.

Even the large Swedish cities have a feel of the open air about them. Here the harbour of Göteborg, Sweden's second largest city, combines waterside housing and pleasure boating with Scandinavia's largest working harbour.

The Swedes call the sea to the east the 'Inland Sea' because it is not very salty or rough, while the North Sea, which laps at the shores of the west coast, has wilder weather. The southwestern coast has the waters of the Kattegat, the strip of water between Sweden and Denmark, to line its beaches, and has gentle seas. The sea has always affected Sweden greatly because it is so dependent on it, but in addition there are also hundreds of lakes in Sweden.

Perhaps the most distinctive feature of Sweden is how unspoilt it is in comparison with other European countries. More than half the land is forest and less than one-tenth of it is cultivated. That which is cultivated has relatively few people settled on it; 8.9 million inhabitants in 450,000 kilometres of land makes for an average of under 20 inhabitants per square kilometre. However, when you're in the heart of Stockholm it certainly feels more crowded than that!

WHAT MAKES SWEDEN SWEDISH?

The answer is, naturally, everything about it. Now that you know more about the geography of Sweden, it's time to read on about the rest of it. It's difficult to really understand a country without knowing more about its background and politics, so in the following chapters you will find out about Swedish history and politics, especially its famed 'Middle Way,' between capitalism and communism, which for years was considered to have struck the balance. In recent times more problems have emerged with the Swedish way, which we will also look at.

The Swedes themselves make Sweden what it is, and so there is a chapter on Swedish ideals and ideas, as well as male–female relations and the class structure, followed by one on Swedish hobbies and pastimes. If you are moving to Sweden, perhaps the best advice anyone can give you is to learn the language as well as you can. Yes, most Swedes speak English, but understandably prefer Swedish, and you will miss out on a lot of the pleasures of Swedish life if you cannot understand the language. Chapter Five will help you find the best ways to learn and important things to know about the language.

We also take a look at shopping, food, Swedish holidays and the arts – all vital to learning about the country. And finally, since you are moving to Sweden and will live there and probably do business there, there are chapters on doing business in Sweden and on the details of everyday life, from banking and housing to education and medical care.

Learning about Sweden before you move, or in the early days of your life there, will make your stay there less frustrating in the beginning and ultimately much more rewarding. As the Swedes say, *lycka till!* (Good luck, said much more often in Swedish than in English.)

Chapter Two

FROM VIKINGS TO THE SWEDISH MODEL

THE VIKING AGE

Perhaps the best known figures in Scandinavian history are the Vikings – bloodthirsty conquerors who spread across western Europe, to Greenland, down to the Caspian Sea and even to North America. Between A.D. 800 and 1050 the land that is now Sweden was ruled by different Viking chieftains in different areas. Although their reputation is of warlike violent men, intent on conquest, their main aim was often trade and they had trade contacts as far away as India and China. As their trading grew more successful they grew greedier and they started to pillage many of the countries they had earlier traded with.

They had two main advantages over the peoples whose lands they ravaged. Firstly they had developed ships which could be sailed or rowed, and were often small enough to be carried between rivers on land. The ships' flat bottoms meant they could sail very close to shore and yet the larger ships could carry up to 50 crew members with supplies to last for more than a month at sea. Secondly, death in battle was nothing to fear for a Viking. They believed that those who died in battle went to Valhalla, the Hall of the Gods, and gained eternal life. The Viking religion was polytheistic, with Odin the master of Valhalla, Thor the god of weather, Frej the fertility god and Balder the god of goodness and wisdom among the most important. Many of the old beliefs and stories are widely read today in collections of Norse mythology, both in Swedish and in English.

The Viking Legacy

Many of the Vikings who travelled overseas left their mark in the form of Nordic placenames – many British town names have Scandinavian roots, and even Normandy, in France, was known originally as the land of the *Norrman*, or men from the north. The Vikings who travelled west were mostly Danish and Norwegian; the Swedish Vikings concentrated on the east, and voyaged the great Russian rivers down to Constantinople and even to Baghdad and Bokhara to bring back riches. Called *Rus* by the local people, they gave the name of *Ryssland*, or Russia to the area they travelled through, and left other names for cities along the way.

Their written language was that of runes, which they inscribed on stones when they documented battles and deaths, and also on arrow-heads, jewellery and other goods. Many runestones are still found around Sweden, with the oldest, from around A.D. 200, in Gotland.

As more Vikings travelled in Christian lands, and brought back Christian slaves, more and more of them converted to the new religion. By 1008 the king, Olof Skötkonung, was baptised – the beginning of the end for the old religions and for the Viking Age.

The Swedish Viking history is that of a proud and fierce trading and warring people. This ancient monument tells the tale of Viking life; both battleships and traders are depicted. It is hard to reconcile such a bloodthirsty history with the peacefulness that is Sweden today.

CHRISTIANITY AND THE MIDDLE AGES

Olof Skötkonung united the two tribes of Sweden, the *Sveas* and the *Götes* and the country became Christian by the middle of the 12th century, though many of the people held to the old beliefs of trolls, fairies and beings living in the woods. Parts of southern Sweden were still part of Denmark, and parts of western Finland today were then part of Sweden.

The Church became stronger and wealthier in the years to follow, and had a very powerful influence over people's lives. It also introduced the Latin alphabet into Sweden, as the Bible and other religious literature were all written in Latin. But the biggest change during the Middle Ages was the emergence of the state as an entity, raising taxes to build fortresses, buy land and equip the military.

The nobility built up power during the Middle Ages and divisions between the nobility, the Church and the peasant workers grew. By the end of the Middle Ages four distinct classes, which became political groupings, had emerged: the nobility, the clergy, the merchants or burghers and the peasants.

During the 13th and 14th centuries trade grew between Sweden and the Hanseatic League in Germany, and at the end of the 14th century a German duke, a distant relation to a former Swedish king, became king of Sweden. He was not popular with the Swedes, and Queen Margareta of Denmark and Norway (which was one country at the time) was asked to intervene to remove him. In 1389 she won a battle over the German-Swedish king and was declared regent of Sweden.

In 1397 the Kalmar Union, between Denmark/Norway and Sweden was formed, and Erik of Pomerania, Margareta's great-nephew, was named king of Sweden. However, Margareta was still regent of Sweden and held the Union together with plans for a United Nordic Union which would act cooperatively. Unfortunately, after her death in 1412 King Erik concentrated more on expanding the Union, and waged many costly and unpopular wars against Germany.

The Swedish peasant leader Engelbrekt, from Dalarna, led a rebellion against this Danish domination in 1434. He was murdered and later honoured as a saint, but the union had foundered by 1448 in a mire of disorder, civil unrest and fighting.

GUSTAV VASA 1521–1611

In the early 16th century the Danish King Christian II attempted to recreate the union by force, but was defeated by Gustav Vasa, the leader who finally established Sweden as an independent power, which it has remained since 1523.

The story of how he came to power is a legend in Sweden. He survived the Danish murder of most of the Swedish nobility in Stockholm and fled to Dalarna to gain support from the peasants there. They were initially reluctant and he started off on skis to Norway, a fugitive from the powerful Danes. When the peasants changed their minds and decided to support him, they followed him on their skis, caught him up and told him they would fight with him. This race through Dalarna is recreated every March with the Vasaloppet, an 86 kilometre cross-country skiing competition with thousands of participants.

Gustav Vasa was elected king in 1523 and, as he needed money badly, set about breaking the power of the Catholic Church with the Reformation. He then became the head of state and Church, Sweden became a Protestant country, and the New Testament was published in Swedish in 1526. There were of course many other contributory factors to the break with Rome; Sweden had been affected by many of the winds of change blowing in Germany and the beliefs adopted were Lutheran, not Anglican.

In Catholic Småland, Nils Dacke led a rebellion against the new king but the rebellion was crushed by the military and ended with Dacke's death in 1543. Since Gustav Vasa's time the Swedish crown has always been inherited rather than elected, although the current royal family does not trace its roots back further than the 19th century.

After Gustav Vasa's death in 1560, King Erik XIV inherited the throne. He is often called Sweden's Renaissance King, and spent much time rebuilding and adding to castles and encouraging arts and sciences. He was dethroned and imprisoned due to the constant power struggles in the royal family, and his brother Johan III succeeded him. Legend has it that Johan III poisoned his brother's pea soup, and that no member of the Swedish royal family has eaten pea soup since!

Johan's son Sigismund reigned after his death from 1592 to 1599, but Gustav Vasa's third son, Karl IX, ruled until his death in 1611. During these years the power of the Hanseatic League was broken, Lutheranism was confirmed by the Uppsala Assembly of 1593, and Estonia became Swedish.

THE TIME OF GREAT POWER 1611-1718

In 1611 Gustav II Adolf, the 'Lion of the North,' succeeded to the throne and led Sweden into her imperial period. Napoleon considered this king to be the equal of Hannibal, Alexander and Caesar on the battlefield, and he entered into the Thirty Years War and won major victories. He was popular, particularly amongst the clergy, but his reign was a hard time for the peasants who had higher taxes to pay and also had to fight the wars. However, Gustav II Adolf also taxed the nobility heavily and expanded the power of Sweden greatly. By the time he died in battle in Lützen, Germany in 1632, Sweden had control over Finland and much of the Baltic states.

Queen Kristina, who succeeded her father, became queen at the age of six. She reigned until 1654, but abdicated the throne after converting to Catholicism, which was an outrage to a country which had fought so many wars against Catholic countries.

The end of Sweden's imperial age, or 'Great Power Time' as it is referred to in Sweden, came after the reign of Karl XII, who tried to force a peace with Russia and lost badly at the battle of Poltava in 1709. He was a legendary fighter but became very unpopular amongst the average Swede because of his constant and expensive warmongering. He was killed in Norway in 1718, shot in the head with a gold bullet, as it was rumoured an ordinary bullet would not kill him. Although when he came to power Sweden had a great many provinces and much influence, and when he died Sweden had lost all the provinces except Finland and Pomerania, Karl XII is still revered by many right wing and nationalist groups in Sweden, who mark November 29, the date of his death, with marches every year.

THE TIME OF FREEDOM 1718–1772
After 1721 the king lost political power and the country was ruled by the *Riksdag,* or parliament. Two parties, the Hats and the Caps, shared power for much of the century, until Gustav III took over in an absolutist coup in 1772. The country was in need of a strong leader, but Gustav III ruled as a dictator, which did not make him popular among the nobility.

THE GUSTAVIAN PERIOD 1772–1809
Nonetheless, the Gustavian Period was Sweden's Enlightenment, a time when the king brought French culture and philosophical ideas to his court. He established the Swedish Academy and a new interest grew in literature, theatre and opera. He ensured the reform of the Swedish language, so that it was purged of many foreign words, and the first Swedish dictionary was published. Religious freedom and a new interest in education for all grew during his reign. Various scientists such as Carl von Linné (Linneaus, the botanist) and C. W. Scheele (the chemist), flourished during this time.

However, his manner of rule proved so unpopular that in 1792 he was assassinated, appropriately for him, while at the opera in fancy dress. A conspiracy of aristocrats had arranged it, and an officer named Anckarström carried it out.

At the beginning of the 19th century, Sweden lost Finland to Russia and traded Swedish Pomerania with Denmark for Norway. Gustav III's successor, Gustav IV Adolf, was deposed in an aristocratic coup in 1809 and replaced with his uncle. In the same year the country adopted a new constitution which was maintained until 1975. It divided legislative powers between the king and the Riksdag, and created the post of ombudsman as a check on the powers of the bureaucracy. This paved the way for modern democracy in Sweden.

THE BERNADOTTES 1810–1844

When the king died in 1814 without an heir, Sweden looked to France, to Marshal Jean-Baptiste Bernadotte, one of Napoleon's soldiers, to take the crown. He took the name Karl XIV Johan and, although he never learned Swedish, was a popular ruler until his death in 1844. He helped restore Swedish self respect after a long period of wars and unrest by establishing the policy of neutrality and working towards Nordic cooperation. This began with the Peace Treaty of Kiel in 1814, which created a Swedish-Norwegian union which was to last until 1905. The current royal family is descended directly from the Bernadotte line.

Läckö Castle dates from the 12th century, but most of these walls are from the 17th. The division between nobility and peasants in Sweden was deep and the rise of a significant middle class did not occur until the 19th century.

INDUSTRIALISATION AND EMIGRATION

Throughout the 19th century the population increased dramatically, from 2.4 million in 1810 to 3.5 million in 1850 and 4.6 million in 1880. Swedes say this was due to 'peace, potatoes and vaccine,' all of which had been unknown in Sweden previously. It was probably also partly to do with land reform, which took place in 1827 and gathered small parcels of land into more economic and efficient units. Agricultural output therefore went up, but the old social fabric began to disappear, scattering villagers to the cities and many abroad.

Reforms continued throughout the century, with *folkskolor* for universal education (for boys) set up in 1842, and a *Riksdagsreform* in 1866 which changed the parliament into a bicameral system and gave voting rights to all property owners. The Industrial Age came to Sweden in the 1870s with main industries in timber, iron and steel, textiles and glass. The Swedish companies ASEA, Ericsson, SKF and AGA were all founded in this time and such inventors as John Ericsson (the rotary propeller) and Alfred Nobel (dynamite and later benefactor of the Nobel prizes) thrived. A new social class based on industrial workers began to grow, and by the end of the century only 50% of the population still earned their living through agriculture.

The Rise of Unionism

As industrial workers grew in number, they formed unions, and a number of other movements, such as the temperance and the women's movements gained popularity. All of these movements have influenced modern Sweden greatly, though it is perhaps the labour movement which was the most widespread. The year 1879 saw the first strike in Sundsvall, and from then on workers joined unions to try and get better working conditions and pay for themselves and their colleagues. Many of the employers pursued union organisers and attempted to stop them by force, sometimes with support from the government. Often unionists were forced to emigrate in fear of their lives.

They were far from alone: more than one million Swedes emigrated, mostly to the United States, during the years 1850 to 1920. In the beginning this was often purely to escape the grinding poverty still prevalent in the countryside and the famine from several years of bad harvests in the 1850s. However, the Church of Sweden was still very strong and many wanted to have greater freedom of religion while others were escaping political problems. Conscription was introduced in 1901 to guard against Russian aggression and many men left Sweden to avoid military service. Emigration had the effect of depleting some villages, especially in Småland, and of setting up large Swedish settlements in the midwest of the United States.

THE EARLY 20TH CENTURY

By 1900, 70% of the population still lived in the country but the move to urban areas was increasing all the time. Unions were also gaining power and the political parties of the 20th century have their roots in these days. The Social Democrats were founded in 1889 and the *Landsorganisation* (LO), the biggest union, which today has over two million members, 90% of whom are blue collar, was founded in 1898. As a countermeasure, the Swedish Employers Federation (SAF) was founded in 1902 but the momentum of the unions was growing and in 1909 there was a nationwide strike over proposed wage cuts. Meanwhile all men over the age of 24 won the right to vote in 1909, and by 1921 women could also vote.

Since then the country has been a modern, industrialised society, with democratic elections to the Riksdag, which leads the nation. In 1920 the first Social Democratic regime was elected to power, with Hjalmar Branting as prime minister. It has always been the biggest party in the Riksdag since then and has held power for 70 years, with breaks in the 1920s, the 1970s and the 1990s when coalition governments were in power. (Coalition governments also ruled during World War II and briefly in the 1950s, but the prime minister in both of those governments was still a Social Democrat.)

Folkhem – The Welfare State

The Social Democrats began to set up a *Folkhem*, or 'People's Home' to ensure that Swedes would not have to suffer extreme poverty again, after the Great Depression of the 1930s. The Depression was felt keenly in Sweden, especially as demand for iron and timber, Sweden's biggest exports, fell away.

The *Folkhem* was built on the foundation of unemployment benefits in 1934, and rose steadily through the years with pensions for all in 1946, child benefit payments in 1947, health insurance for all in 1955, pensions with extra payment for workers in 1959, compulsory nine years of schooling in 1962 and parental leave in 1974. The ideal was to prevent problems, rather than cure them, and to eliminate poverty. After the insecurity and extreme poverty of the average Swede in the centuries before, the goal of creating an ideal environment for living was one that most Swedes were willing to support through high taxation. As a result, Sweden became the first country in the world where doctors could not tell the social class of a child by examining his or her physical health. The system worked so well that no matter what your profession, your child was guaranteed good medical care and you received special payments to ensure you could feed, clothe and shelter your family adequately. A complete welfare state is expensive to maintain, but as Sweden's economy and wealth continued to grow in the first half and middle of the 20th century, the problem of financing the social benefits did not arise until much later.

NEUTRALITY AND PEACEMAKERS

Sweden stayed out of both World War I and World War II because of its policy of neutrality, maintained since 1814. In World War I Norway and Denmark maintained a united front with Sweden and many Scandinavians volunteered as Red Cross workers. The war years were difficult for Sweden because of food and fuel shortages – a deciding factor in the election of the first Social Democratic government in 1920.

In 1939, the Finnish-Russian Winter War tested Swedish neutrality and 12,000 Swedish volunteers fought on the Finnish side. Many Finnish children were evacuated to Sweden during this war – and many stayed throughout the Second World War and then afterwards.

In World War II Sweden stood alone as a neutral state after Denmark and Norway were invaded by German forces. This was a decision important to Swedes, who did not want to abandon their neutral principles, but it was a decision for which many Norwegians have yet to forgive Sweden. In the early war years Sweden provided iron ore to the Nazis as a normal trading power, as well as to the Allies, also normal trading partners. However, the infamous Transport Agreement of 1940, signed by Per Albin Hansson as a way of safeguarding Sweden against German invasion, allowed over 140,000 German troops to travel through Sweden enroute to occupied Norway and to Finland (after Finland allied itself with Germany against the Soviet Union).

The Transport Agreement ended in 1943, to the relief of most Swedes. Many Swedes could not stay uninvolved in the conflict on a non-military basis. One hero of the time was Raoul Wallenberg, the Swedish diplomat in Prague, who bent the rules to issue Swedish passports to Jews and other victims of the Nazis. Another was Count Folke Bernadotte, who received the official Nazi surrender from Himmler and negotiated the release of thousands of concentration camp prisoners in 1945. Bernadotte's white buses, as they were called, travelled up from Germany saving mostly Norwegian and Danish prisoners, but taking as many others as possible along the way.

Throughout the 20th century, Sweden has maintained its neutrality and promoted international cooperation and aid through its financial, legal and personal contributions. The peacemakers after World War II include Count Folke Bernadotte, who agreed to mediate between the Jews and Arabs in Palestine for the Security Council of the UN, and was assassinated there in 1948. Another great figure was Dag Hammarskjöld, the second secretary general of the United

Nations from 1953 to 1961. He too died while working for peace, though in his case death came in a plane crash in Africa while he was trying to resolve the crisis in the Congo. Both of these figures contributed to Sweden's international image as peace brokers, which Alfred Nobel had started in 1895 by establishing the Nobel Peace Prize.

The tradition of working internationally towards peace continued in the 1970s and 1980s with the work of Olof Palme as a negotiator in the Iran-Iraq war, and as a voice for the Third World. Even today many Third World nations look to Sweden for aid and justice; Sweden is one of the most generous benefactors of aid to less fortunate countries, relative to size. SIDA, the Swedish aid organisation, distributes aid worldwide, and the story goes that some nations think of Sweden as one of the world's superpowers because so much of their aid comes with the blue and yellow flag painted on it. In the 1990s the amount of aid has decreased but the tradition of giving continues, as does the tradition of peacemakers – former prime minister, Carl Bildt worked as a mediator in the war in the conflict in Bosnia in the mid-1990s.

Neutrality and Militarism

Sweden's neutrality does not mean, however, that it has abandoned military training and spending. Quite the opposite; there is compulsory military service for all men and a large defence budget. Neutrality means that Sweden cannot rely on any other country to defend it because it belongs to no alliances. In spite of its peace-loving reputation, Sweden supports a thriving arms trade, partly because otherwise it could not afford to arm itself for defence. This double edged sword of neutrality makes many Swedes uncomfortable, and there are many who protest against the arms trade.

Nevertheless, many perceive the arms buildup as a necessary evil and while, from the perspective of the current situation, an invasion of Sweden seems unlikely, a Soviet invasion was a very real fear during the Cold War. At one point a Soviet submarine was discovered stranded on rocks in the southern Swedish archipelago – giving credence to the belief that the Soviet Union was a real threat.

Both before and since joining the European Union, many Swedes have voiced concerns over plans for a European defence force. Most other EU nations are members of NATO, and while Sweden does volunteer troops to the United Nations Peacekeeping forces, there is little support for joining NATO task forces.

MODERN TIMES

After the Second World War, Sweden's economic strength grew and grew, and so did the welfare state. Growth meant that many immigrant workers were invited in to help swell the labour force and, through the influx of Italians, Greeks and Yugoslavians, Sweden became a little less insular culturally. With influence spreading from the United States through television, and with Sweden's traditional links with central Europe, the hope was that Sweden would carve a middle way between capitalism and communism. Nobody wanted the social divisions inherent in pure capitalism, nor the oppression evident in communist countries. The aggression from both sides of the Iron Curtain turned peace-loving Swedes away.

The government continued to be Social Democratic, and Swedes built up their security and their way of life. It was hardly shaken until the oil crisis in the early 1970s caused unemployment and events in the rest of the world, particularly the war in Vietnam, made Sweden sit up and take notice. In the late 1960s Sweden stopped welcoming immigrants; the needed extra labour had overrun the available jobs. In the 1970s the country learned to cope with high inflation and foreign debts. Partly as a response to this there were wide ranging constitutional and educational reforms. By 1976, after several years of unease, the Social Democrats lost power for the first time in over forty years, and various coalition governments ruled until 1982.

Another issue very much in Swedish minds was how to reduce dependence on the oil producing nations after the oil crisis of the 1970s. Much investment and trust was put into nuclear power. By 1980, when a referendum was held, the effects of Three Mile Island and other nuclear power plant accidents had changed Swedish minds again, and it was agreed to phase the use of nuclear power out over 25 years.

Olof Palme

Olof Palme led the Social Democratic Party back into power in 1982. He was a very controversial figure in Swedish politics, who was prime minister from 1969 to 1976 and again from 1982 to 1986. His open condemnation of the American role in the war in Vietnam earned him the disapproval of the United States (especially after he offered asylum to American draft dodgers) but his work for the United Nations in the Iran-Iraq war won him admiration. At home he was seen as the left wing champion of workers, who himself came from a wealthy upper class family – a hero to those who thought of themselves as working class but a traitor to those who still liked to think of themselves as upper class.

themselves as working class but a traitor to those who still liked to think of themselves as upper class.

On February 28, 1986, as he walked home from the cinema with his wife, an unknown assassin shot him dead. The whole of Sweden was rocked – their self perception as a safe nation, where the prime minister could walk unguarded in the streets of the capital was destroyed. Worse still, the assassin has never been caught. Ten years on, Swedish police are still working on the case. Ingvar Carlsson succeeded Palme as prime minister, and vowed to continue his policies. In the late 1980s, however, Sweden was shaken further by scandals involving politicians, bank and company officials. The obedient nation who trusted in authority learned a degree of disillusionment. In the 1990s this disillusionment only deepened with revelations about forced sterilisation of disabled citizens and possible wartime collaborations between the Wallenberg family and the Nazis in Germany.

Recession and the Welfare State

Not only was it disillusioned, it was about to experience the worst recession since the 1930s. In 1990 Carlsson pushed through various austerity measures, but by the 1991 election the Social Democrats had lost power again, to a right wing coalition led by Carl Bildt and the Conservative Party *(Moderaterna)*. This administration, in power until 1994, set about dismantling many of the structures set up during decades of Social Democrat rule, by privatising state industries and cutting back further on centralised state power and benefits.

These cutbacks were inevitable; the full welfare state had grown too expensive for a nation struggling under recession to fund. The economy worsened in the early 1990s, with unemployment reaching as high as 14% and the currency taking a nose dive. By 1994 the country had voted the Social Democrats back into power, with Ingvar Carlsson back as prime minister. But the country had changed both socially and politically, and the shift to the right has not disappeared.

31

Sweden joined the European Union on January 1, 1995, but only after a referendum which split the country nearly in half. Many of the just under 50% who voted against did so out of concern for diminished environmental and gender equality standards, and still campaign for Sweden to withdraw. The rotating presidency of the EU was Sweden's in 2001, and Persson used it to draw more attention to such issues, as well as trying to get other European nations to adopt such Swedish laws as making television advertising to children illegal.

Ingvar Carlsson resigned as prime minister on February 28, 1996, ten years to the day after Palme's assassination, when he first took office. His successor, Goran Persson, has since led the country through both the 1998 and 2002 parliamentary elections, though with a reduced majority. Although the conservative parties lost votes in the 2002 elections, more Swedes voted for the smaller parties than before.

THE POLITICAL SYSTEM

Sweden is a constitutional monarchy, but since the reforms of 1975 the monarch, although head of state, has no political power at all. Until 1971 the parliament (Riksdag) was bicameral, but reforms in that year led to a unicameral legislature of 350 elected members.

In 1975 the constitution was revised for the first time in over 150 years. The foundations of the constitution are representative democracy, popular sovereignty and parliamentarianism. The Riksdag was decreased to 349 members to prevent tie votes. Elections are held every four years (until 1995 it was every three years) and places are won through a system of proportional democracy. A party must win at least 4% of the nationwide vote or 12% of a regional vote to be represented in the Riksdag. Every Swedish citizen aged 18 or over is eligible to vote; 90% do.

Political Parties

There are seven major political parties in the Riksdag today, four parties polled less than 10% of the vote in the 2002 election.

Social Democrats: *Socialdemokraterna*
The leading party, it has its main support amongst the unions, and industrial and blue-collar workers. Their ideology is based on economic democracy, and equal distribution of wealth and power. (144 members after 2002 election.)

Conservatives: *Moderaterna*
The voters for the most right wing party come mostly from high paid white collar workers, and the so-called upper class. They share elements of their philosophy with the British Conservatives and American Republicans, advocating a market economy and a reduced public sector. (55 members after 2002 election.)

Liberals: *Folkpartiet*
The social-liberal ideology of this party includes advocacy of a guided market economy, with political democracy. (48 members after 2002 election.)

Christian Democrats: *Kristdemokraterna*
This party is broadly Christian-Conservative, and was a part of the coalition government in the early 1990s. Voters are attracted to it from across the spectrum, except from the socialist parties. (33 members after 2002 election.)

Left Party: *Vänsterpartiet*
This party is the successor to the Communist Party, and changed its name in the early 1990s after the fall of many Communist regimes in Europe. It campaigns for a planned, socialist economy based on state ownership. Many of the voters are highly educated white collar workers, although the traditional voter base was the working class. (30 members after 2002 election.)

Centre Party: *Centern*
The former Agrarian Party's main voter base is among farmers. They favour free enterprise, decentralisation of power and an end to nuclear energy. (22 members after 2002 election.)

Ecology Party: *Miljöpartiet*

Also called the Green Party, the Ecology Party is one of the youngest parties, founded in 1982, and attracts many young voters who see protection of the environment as one of the main issues facing Sweden today. (17 members after 2002 election.)

THE OMBUDSMAN AND OPENNESS

An important Swedish contribution to the world has been the ombudsman, an official appointed by the government to investigate complaints against public authorities. This empowers citizens and guards against abuse of power by any officials or governmental bodies. There are many different levels of ombudsmen in Sweden, but the main ones are elected by the Riksdag and cover complaints against the justice system (JO) and in cases of ethnic discrimination (DO) and children's rights (BO). There are in fact four ombudsmen for justice, one of whom acts as the head ombudsman. If you have been unfairly treated by a public authority you should always begin by complaining to the authority itself. If you still feel the case is unresolved, contact the relevant ombudsman.

Another particular feature of Swedish political life is the principle of open government. While the government may keep certain documents secret if they are matters of national security, other documents must be available to the general public if requested. In practice this means that you can request to see any records concerning you, and you must be allowed to see the records. Sweden's policy of openness is causing some problems with fellow members of the European Union, who keep such documents secret in their own countries.

Fairness and Justice

The history of Sweden travels from a deeply divided and class ridden society with the vast majority of people scraping a living from the land, to a society committed to equality and a high standard of living for all. In recent years economic recession and changes in society forced Swedes to reassess how they want to be governed, and what is important to them.

Today's Swede is still attached to the land, but lives a very modern life, with all the technological advances which make life comfortable. The country still adheres to neutrality and peacemaking, donating aid to Third World countries and welcoming refugees, but it worries about the cost of it all. A sense of fairness and justice still motivates the Swedish people, even if today the interpretation of what is fair may vary amongst them.

SWEDEN TODAY

Sweden today is a nation which is still trying to tread the middle ground, while succeeding in the modern post-Cold War world. The principles of fairness and equality are not lightly brushed aside from the Swedish psyche, but the cost of maintaining the cradle to grave welfare system is proving too high. Still professing neutrality, Sweden is cooperating with many non-neutral nations on defence issues – compromising its neutrality in the opinion of many.

Nevertheless, aspects of the welfare system are looked upon with envy by many other countries. In today's Sweden, even while welfare benefits are being cut back, Swedes receive subsidised medical and dental care, housing benefit if needed, unemployment benefit if needed, free schooling, child benefit, up to a year's paid parental leave, subsidised elderly care, subsidised child care, free medical and dental treatment for children, and subsidies to help people who cannot work or support themselves.

For this Swedes still pay very high taxes, though the extremely high levels famous in the 1960s and 1970s have fallen to levels similar to other European nations. Some people try to cheat the system by occasionally working black, or hiding their savings accounts abroad. The desire to get the better of the system is not new, but perhaps the disillusionment behind it originates only from the past fifteen years.

Sweden faces many changes in society, and such challenges as the rising rate of crime and violence, high unemployment rates, the new popularity of some right wing nationalist groups and even homelessness have no proven methods of cure. Sweden has not often had to face these challenges.

On the positive side, it's important to remember that the crime rate in Sweden is very low, and even a considerable increase will not reach the levels of many other Western nations. But other principles in Swedish life, such as strict freedom of speech and openness, mean that certain shifts are much more noticeable than in other nations. One example is of nationalist groups, who are allowed to recruit members and apply for the government grants available for associations. The groups are still a tiny minority and Swedes are divided as to whether the danger they pose is great enough to abandon principles of fairness established in better economic times.

— *Chapter Three* —

THE SWEDISH PEOPLE

SWEDISH CHARACTERISTICS

According to Baedeker's guidebook, the Scandinavians "tend to be quiet and unassuming, patient themselves and offended by impatience in others. Their honesty, hospitality and helpfulness are proverbial." It is true that the general character of the Swedes is similar to that of the other Scandinavians, and is shaped by a common history, language roots, climate and geography. Swedes, however, are often seen as more cosmopolitan and industrious than the Norwegians, and quieter and more reserved than the Danes. Respectability and a quiet life are very important to most Swedes, even though many rebel against this in their youth. Swedes themselves often joke about this; as soon as you have acquired the trappings of respectability and being settled (a terraced house, two children, a dog and a red Volvo estate car) you are called a 'Real Svensson' and fit right in!

They joke also about the differences between them and other Scandinavians. For example, there was an advertisement on Swedish television for a lottery game called Viking Lotto, which shows the reactions of winners from Norway, Denmark, Finland and Sweden. The Norwegians are kitted out in bright jumpers and are on cross-country skis, singing loudly and happily. The Danes are out at a restaurant, celebrating lustily with food and drink, while the Finns are raucously shouting and chasing each other around a sauna with birch twigs. Meanwhile, the Swede who wins is sitting on the couch in his living room, surrounded by his family. As the winning numbers come on the television, he says in a moderately pleased voice, "Well, it looks like I won." His wife says, "Well done" and smiles to herself, and the family settles back to watching television. And when you have spent some time in Sweden you can imagine this happening!

There are many ways to describe the character of the Swedes; some stem from history, others from the difficulty of living in a harsh climate and others from societal norms and expectations. It is important to remember that there will always be many exceptions to every description, but many Swedes will fit in to the descriptions.

Rural Roots

Until 1870 fewer than 10% of the population lived in urban areas. This means that almost all Swedes have very recent roots in the country-side, and spend their holidays in small cottages (*stugor*) in the country near where they, their parents and/or their grandparents grew up. Many Swedes are interested in folk culture and environmentalism because of this connection but, perhaps more importantly, the average Swede possesses a quiet pragmatism gained from generations on the land. They respect their old traditions, even if many of them no longer live by them. It is a quality that manages to sit comfortably with the modern and sophisticated attitude that Swedes also possess because, perhaps, both of these attitudes are based on a love of simplicity and directness.

Modern and Efficient

This juxtaposition of sophistication and a love of the simple rural life stems from Swedish history. Although Swedes are traditionally rural, they are also traders going back to Viking times, and have been industrialists for the past 130 years. They are often seen as harder, colder, more efficient and less relaxed when compared to their Scandinavian neighbours. One way in which they do not differ is in their belief in improving life through modernity.

Swedes enjoy using modern conveniences and pride themselves on having a modern and liberal outlook on life. They like to work efficiently and take time off when the work is done. Leaving work on time does not mean Swedes dislike work or don't work hard; they simply believe that there is a time and place for work, play and family life. In fact, work is very important to most Swedes and, in common with many other Western cultures, they often define themselves through their work.

Punctuality

Their efficiency extends to a fastidious desire for punctuality. If you are coming from the UK or the US you might think you know what they mean; it's easy to get impatient with people from some cultures who are more laid back. But Swedes are more punctual than even the average Brit or American, and it extends beyond the workplace to their home life as well. Much at work and home is planned, organised and scheduled carefully, and it can throw the whole schedule off if something is delayed. They are sticklers for fairness, and as they would not keep you waiting, they are surprised if you keep them waiting – even if it is just for ten minutes. At first this may seem a little extreme to you, but when you realise that it is part of the Swedish respect for other people's time, you will probably want to adopt it yourself.

Spontaneity is not a high priority to a Swede and nor is improvising. This is partly due to the inherent cautiousness which stems from years of poverty (and perhaps a fear that they are not too far removed from it!) For foreigners who see Sweden as very wealthy it seems extraordinary that Swedes can be so worried about being poor, but the wealth is too recently acquired to allow Swedes to be comfortable with it yet.

A note concerning punctuality and business – keeping someone waiting to intimidate them, as happens in many other cultures, does not work at all in Sweden. It only serves to make the Swede believe that you are extremely rude and probably very badly brought up. If kept waiting for too long he or she may just arrange to reschedule with your secretary, defeating your whole purpose.

Attached to this desire for efficiency and modernity comes a materialism similar to American materialism. Swedes like their dishwashers, mobile phones, electric bread bakers and so on. Such conveniences as central heating, televisions, microwave ovens and washing machines are more or less taken for granted now and in fact central heating and televisions are considered a necessary part of modern living by the government. While Swedes do not like to work overtime as a rule, money is relatively important to them (if only to pay for the extras) and money-consciousness is another common characteristic of Swedes.

Reserved and Quiet

The quiet Swede is a very common stereotype, and often a very valid one. Naturally you will meet many gregarious and talkative Swedes, but you are unlikely to have many problems getting a word in edgewise at a meeting or dinner party. Swedes sometimes say that every conversation lasts seven minutes; after that it peters out until a new one starts. Sometimes the new one begins immediately but often there is a companionable silence before the next one.

It is said in many countries that politics, religion and sex are no-go areas of conversation. In a way this is also true in Sweden (except perhaps sex, about which Swedes are less embarrassed than most).

The weather, money and sports are very common topics. Politics is discussed but it is rare for anyone to openly discuss his or her own political inclination. Swedes are not very good at small talk, they prefer to get directly to the point, without being confrontational of course. If it is impossible to be direct without a confrontation a Swede will often remain silent.

The expression 'silence implies consent' does not work at all in Sweden – in fact it may be quite the opposite. A Swede may want to contradict you, but be too reserved or afraid of being rude to do so, and remain quiet. On the other hand if he or she agrees with you, you will probably hear about it!

Åke Daun, an ethnologist at Stockholm University, wrote in a *National Geographic* article that: "Swedes are a painfully shy people. We're taught very early not to stand out from the crowd or risk making anyone uncomfortable." He compares his own society to that of Japan in its emphasis on quiet conformity.

The reserved Swede is happier socialising with a group of good friends. Here Swedes enjoy eating outdoors – which they do whenever they have the opportunity. Silence at the dinner table does not make a Swede uncomfortable.

This comparison continues in the Swedish (and Japanese) dislike of showing their feelings. Although Swedes generally prefer to be straightforward, and believe that being open is very important, this does not extend necessarily to private or emotional issues. Swedes are often very isolated socially, with extended families living apart from one another. There is no pub or cafe tradition, no congregating in open areas and often, people do not even know their own neighbours. Instead, Swedes tend to socialise with friends from school, work, or sports or special interest organisations. However, their lives are often so full of activities, like work, holidays and home improvements that most everyday social interaction usually centres around the nuclear family.

Naturally no one can say that this is either a bad or a good thing, but it can be very lonely for immigrants to Sweden until they get used to it. Indeed, it is very lonely for many Swedes – the high rate of suicide (15th among reporting nations) is sometimes linked to loneliness and to an inability or unwillingness to share emotional problems. It is also linked to the long winters, and to the higher rate of reporting suicide in Sweden than in other countries, so it's important not to read too much into the social isolation aspect of this type of statistic.

Service Equals Subservience

One way in which Swedes are not at all like the Japanese is in their attitude towards service. While the Japanese are very service-minded, in Sweden this is seen as almost subservient as well as superficial and, as all Swedes are meant to be equal, this makes them uncomfortable. Swedish shop workers, waiters and salespeople are often very friendly and can be helpful, but you will not often see the same standard of service as in Japan or the United States (on the other hand, Brits will feel right at home).

Shop Talk

Swedes have also been called rude and abrupt by foreigners used to different ways. This can be partly attributed to differences in the language but also, again, to the Swedish preference for directness and efficiency. A Swede does not want to use two words when one would suffice. Not only is it a waste of time and energy, but they think of it as purely superficial as well.

For example, to buy a newspaper in Sweden requires perhaps six words:

Jag tar den här – "I'll take this," waving the paper, followed by:

Trettio – "Thirty" and then by:

Tack – "Thank you" (This is optional.)

If you have to actually ask for the paper it takes even fewer words – simply say the name of the paper and hand over the money (a Swede will probably already know the cost anyhow). To buy a newspaper in England, on the other hand, can drive a Swede to absolute distraction. Start by asking for the paper, please. The newsagent will reply with the price, please. Hand over the money with a thank you. He/she hands back the change and the paper with another thank you. Take the change and the paper with a third thank you and goodbye. The newsagent says goodbye as well. This means at least nine extra words as far as a Swede is concerned – just think of the waste, and no one benefits from this! Better just to do the job and get on with it.

This desire for direct speech and as little of it as possible led to frustrations between the Swedish and French workers who held meetings in the early 1990s when Volvo and Renault considered a merger. The Swedish workers complained that the meetings took far too long on preliminaries and formalities, and that once they got down to business they couldn't get a word in because the French dominated the conversation. As Swedes abhor interrupting, they waited for the natural pause in the conversation. Not surprisingly, it never came. (There were no doubt frustrations of an opposite nature amongst the French along the lines of, "They never contribute, we do it all!")

43

Seriousness

Swedes take life seriously. They work hard and are generally loyal to their job and to their company, and they take pride in the work they do. A refreshing difference between Sweden and many other countries is that there is respect for work across the spectrum of jobs; from a factory worker to a teacher, or a bus driver to a doctor, Swedes take pride in their work and strive to do well.

Honest and Reliable

It is impossible to say that a national characteristic of one country is to be more honest or reliable than another but Swedes do take the concept of being 'fair' very seriously, and honesty is considered an important part of this. So too is reliability – it is not fair to go back on your word or to agree to do something and not do it.

Honesty and reliability are important parts of speaking directly and being open about things (except, of course, private or emotional things). The idea of saving face, common in some Muslim and Asian countries, is not as common in Sweden. On the other hand, a Swede will rarely think or reason aloud, as an American might. Swedes will either answer directly or else keep quiet until it's all clear in their own minds and then answer directly. The time delay in answering can seem like prevarication, but it's more likely to be Swedish caution. It wouldn't do to go back on what has been said, so it had better be correct the first time.

A Dry Sense of Humour

Because of their reserve and lack of open emotion, Swedes are often considered to be humourless and inhibited socially. Another Scandinavian joke (told by Swedes on themselves) is that of two Danes, Norwegians, Finns and Swedes stranded on four separate islands. By the time they are all rescued the Danes have set up a cooperative, the Norwegians are out fishing, the Finns have cut down all the trees and the Swedes are still waiting to be introduced.

Fortunately this is a slight exaggeration! Swedes are not generally this inhibited and, although a bit of alcohol helps them relax (and the young sometimes rely on this heavily), they will generally be comfortable with people they haven't met before quicker than you think. It is not unusual for Swedes who are giving a party to either start the party with a game to break the ice, or else to have a seating plan at a dinner party to force people to speak with people they don't know. "We know ourselves," one Swede told me, "and otherwise we would only talk with the people we came with or have known for years."

They share a similar sense of humour to the British, in common with their reserve, and a lot of British comedy programmes and comedians travel easily to Sweden. Such programmes as "Fawlty Towers" (a British production with John Cleese) are as well loved in Sweden as in the UK, and many Swedish comedians and programmes follow the same vein of very dry humour. American humour is often considered to be a little too unsubtle and slapstick and, oddly enough, Swedes seem to be proud of that.

It is said that Swedes find it hard to laugh at themselves. You may think this peculiar, judging by the jokes they tell about themselves.

TRIGG.

The truth is probably more that they can poke fun at themselves but they do not find it at all amusing if a foreigner does. This is common with most nations, but one difference is that Swedes really believe that there is a right way to do things, and they have found it. Therefore no foreigner ought to laugh about it, even misguidedly, as a Swede would assume.

Smugness

This leads to one of the charges often levelled at Swedes. They are smug, always believing their way is better and therefore they are better. Many Swedes travel abroad for their holidays, and there are a lot of foreign news and travel programmes on television, which leads Swedes to believe they are better informed about the lower standards of living in other nations, and confirms their superiority. Then again, they are far from being the only people convinced of their own superiority.

Peter Watcyn-Jones, a Brit who lived and taught in Sweden for many years, sums up the Swedish character in his English teaching book *What Next?* by describing a Swede as "usually punctual, honest, reliable, clean, has his own teeth and is law-abiding." In addition, "he is shy, reserved, serious, industrious and finds it hard to laugh at himself." Watcyn-Jones meant his essay to be used while teaching Swedes English, and it is meant to be ironic, but many of my Swedish students agreed with all he had said about them – it hit the mark more accurately than intended.

SEPARATION OF AGE GROUPS

Sweden is a very homogenous country by nature, but an important part of its society has been its socialisation of different age groups. Monica Rabe, in her book *Living and Working in Sweden*, points out that one can divide the population into six age groups, which follow their own paths, with little interaction between them and other age groups.

Small Children

Children up to the age of 6 are not in full time schooling, but most go to either child minders (*dagmamma* or day-mother) or to play- or preschool. Since the vast majority of Swedish parents work, few children are at home with their parents after the age of 18 months, unless they have a younger sibling. Even then, many children will go to playgroups; it is considered better for the children to learn to socialise and make friends than to be at home.

School Children

From the age of 6 or 7, for at least nine years, children are in full time compulsory schooling. After school, many go to special activities, ranging from sports teams and scouts to piano lessons and extra language coaching. Those whose parents work full time often go to a 'free time home' after school, where they can play and be looked after by trained carers until their parents come to fetch them after work.

Children gain early independence from their parents and the emphasis for them is on fitting in with their peer groups, rather than with their families.

Young Adults

Although children can leave school after nine years (generally aged 16), 98% of Swedes stay on for the two to three years of *gymnasium* to gain further qualifications, either vocational or in preparation for higher education. It is not unusual for teenagers to move away from home and live alone in flats from the age of 18 and, as not all gymnasiums offer all subjects, many students commute to other towns to study, or for athletic training. Again, at this age the peer group is very important, although not as many Swedes share an apartment with friends as in Anglophone cultures.

Parental supervision and involvement are not as important here as in many other countries. Teenagers decide on a profession from the

Swedish children are encouraged to become independent younger than in many other countries. These Swedish children have come alone to a neighbourhood hill to sled on the early winter snow.

age of 14 or 15, because that will decide which subjects they will study at gymnasium level and whether or not they will continue to higher education or not.

When students are at university it is very rare for them to live at home, and most receive student loans to enable them to rent flats, while many also take part time jobs to help finance themselves. University students tend to be older than those in other countries; they often do not start until they are 20 or older and finish in their late 20s. Until recently, all Swedish men had to do military service for between 8 and 18 months, but this has been relaxed somewhat. A popular option for many is to travel extensively, perhaps around the world or in Africa, or to work or study abroad, often as an au pair to improve language skills, or as a volunteer in a developing country.

Young adults are an important consumer group in Sweden; they often have good salaries and little family responsibility. The average

age at which women have a first child is 28 and men 30, and moving in with a partner (through marriage or not) does not entail the same responsibility as in other countries, as it is assumed that both partners will continue to work. This is one of the most visible age groups, as they are the ones who have the time and money to frequent restaurants, bars and nightclubs.

Families with Children – Barnfamiljar

The majority of Swedes settle down and have 2.1 children (an average which has risen in recent years from 1.6 in 1983) and the years between the late 20s and the mid-40s are often dominated by family life. Between full time jobs, child care and keeping up their standard of living, this group has no extra time for restaurants and going out. Most socialising is done with other *barnfamiljar* in homes. The focus is very much on the family and the home during these years.

The Middle-Aged Group

Middle-age can be anywhere from late 30s to early 60s, and this group tends to have more money and time after their children have left home. Most of the top positions in Swedish firms are taken by people in this group. In recent years, which have been difficult economically, there have been complaints from the younger generations about this group, particularly those called the *40-talisterna*, who were born in the 1940s.

These people benefited entirely from the welfare state built up after the War and, after a period of radicalism in their youth in the 1960s, have now become more conservative. This is not unusual, but what bothers some of the younger generation is that they are still benefiting, while younger Swedes are unlikely to benefit as much throughout their lives from the welfare system. Some say that the *40-talisterna* are like the cork in a bottle – until they move out of the way by retiring the younger generation has no chance of moving up.

Pensioners

The age of retirement in Sweden is 65, although in recent years many have taken early retirement as young as 58, but it is possible to go on working until the age of 70. As life expectancies are greater than in most countries (around 76 for men and 80 for women), Swedish pensioners have a long and often active life after retirement. It is not usual for older parents to live with their children and when they can no longer care for themselves they live in either retirement homes or specially assisted housing for elderly people. If they can still live alone but need some assistance with shopping, cleaning and so on, the state provides help with this.

There is not very much daily interaction between the generations, and while some pensioners will help with baby-sitting, and some children will help care for their aged parents, for the most part they get together only on holidays and for family celebrations. This is similar to the situation in many Western countries, but the division is perhaps sharper in Sweden because the state has been so willing to step in and help.

A presentation at a 60th birthday party. 'Even' birthdays are cause for celebration in Sweden. At 60 it's not time to retire yet, but even past the age of 70 many Swedes are helped to live in their own homes with dignity, by homehelp funded by the state.

LAGOM – JUST ENOUGH

Two of the most important concepts in Swedish society are those of *lagom* and *trygghet*. *Lagom* means 'just enough' and stems from the days of the Vikings. They drank their mead from a common bowl, and it was understood that each man would drink *laget om* – not too little for his own sake but not too much so that all could share.

In a way, Swedes strive towards *lagom* because they strive towards moderation. One should work hard, but not too hard, and eat enough, but not too much, and have enough money, but not too much, and so on. This is part of the reason that so many Swedes have embraced socialist ideas, because they fit in with their ideas of fairness, equality and *lagom*. It is certain that the concept of *lagom* has made for a more harmonious society, but it has also had the effect of discouraging some Swedes to strive beyond 'just enough.'

The ideal of equality and *lagom* has in the past meant a taxation system designed to share the wealth more fairly and therefore evenly. This has sometimes meant that workers who earned overtime received very little extra money for it, and so people became more and more reluctant to work overtime, taking time off in lieu instead. In addition, a promotion with a salary increase was not worth very much financially because the worker would move automatically into a higher tax bracket. The desire for equality worked at times against the ideal of striving for more – the socialist policy often discouraged people from working harder.

Jantelagen – Down by Law

Another discouragement comes through the concept of *Jantelagen*, or *Jante* Law. Swedes share with the Brits and the Australians a dislike for 'tall poppies' or high achievers, and the view that *'lagom* is best' accentuates this. While Australians talk of cutting down their tall poppies, Swedes talk about the *Jante* Law, which, although it is not the law of the land, counsels people to not boast or try to lift themselves above others. The Law goes like this:

1. You shall not believe that you are somebody.
2. You shall not believe that you are as good as we are.
3. You shall not believe that you are smarter than we are.
4. You shall not think that you are better than we are.
5. You shall not believe that you know more than we do.
6. You shall not believe that you are superior to us.
7. You shall not believe that you are good enough.
8. You shall not laugh at us.
9. You shall not believe that anyone cares about you.
10. You shall not believe that you can teach us anything.

(Translation by Monica Rabe)

Many Swedes strive therefore to be much like all the others, to conform and fit in. If a Swede succeeds he sets himself up for envy from his neighbours, friends and family – unless, of course, he succeeds just enough. This often has the effect of encouraging even the brightest students to settle for *lagom* jobs rather than more challenging options. To aim higher would mean that the student thought he or she was better than others and worth more, so it isn't as acceptable. This affects the would-be entrepreneurs, risk takers, artists and inventors as well as the genuinely average student.

The educational system over the past 30 years has not tried to alter this, and has worked hard to instill the values of consensus and cooperation into children. Both of these very worthy ideals often make children see competition as a negative thing, and also see keeping a low profile as a good thing. Average is good, orderly is good. However, recent educational reforms are now working towards keeping egalitarian principles while still catering for and encouraging brighter students.

Lagom is in many ways an excellent concept, and fits in well with the Swedish ideas of fairness. It is likely that it will be more and more challenged as Sweden leaves behind some of its international isolation, and that Swedes, appreciating consensus as they do, will work to incorporate the good aspects of it into their new societal ideas. After all, there are still entrepreneurs, artists, inventors and high achievers in Sweden in spite of the *Jante* Law and *lagom*. And Swedes would probably wish that more countries in the world would practice *lagom* – it would, after all, be fairer.

TRYGGHET – SAFE AND SECURE

Trygghet can be translated into security, or safety, and is a concept very dear to the Swedish heart. Swedes prefer to be cautious and attempt to foresee the risks before committing to a decision. In business they often evaluate and document everything before making their minds up – it's always better to be on the safe side.

As mentioned before, this fits in with the Swedish love of planning and predictability, and also of consensus. In their view it can't be a good decision if there is disagreement about it. If this sounds boring to you, remember that it also fits in with the quality of reliability – once a decision has been made a Swede will generally hold to it, and mean what he or she says.

Part of the ideal behind the People's Home welfare state started from the idea of *trygghet*. The welfare state provides safety from all things uncomfortable or unpleasant and allows Swedes to plan safely and helps ensure a tranquil life for all. Swedes feel more secure when they know exactly what is going to affect them, and this may also be why they speak directly and avoid too much subtlety in conversation.

This directness extends to the government; all documents are open for the public to examine, and you can always be granted access to documents about yourself (such as your health records, police records, etc.) This is important to the Swedish sense of security. It has also caused problems in the European Union recently, when some papers classed as private were released in Sweden, as they must be by law. They were not released into other EU nations, which do not have the same tradition, and there was much embarrassment and confusion over the resolution of the problem.

The Swedish love of safety is evident in the goods in the shops and in the consumer choices they make. The strong safety record of Volvo cars, the stringent factory regulations for worker safety and the plethora of smoke alarms, child safety seats, and other safety items on sale, all point towards it. Seatbelts in both the front and back seats are required in cars in Sweden, and many medicines available over the counter in the US and the UK are prescription only or not even for sale in Sweden. In addition, films and television programmes are often censored for the viewers' sake. These same films are sometimes censored of their sex scenes in the United States. Sweden is comfortable with sex scenes but considers violence in films to be more dangerous than Americans do.

Trygghet is not only freedom from danger and fear, but also a feeling which develops when a Swede feels secure in his or her job, and home and family. For this reason Swedes move around the country less often than Brits or Americans do, and would certainly be loath to move for work reasons, especially later in life. It is also why the recent economic uncertainty has hit Sweden so hard; Swedes have been so used to the *trygghet* of their jobs before the late 1980s that the rising unemployment level probably affected them more than it would have another nation.

THE CLASS SYSTEM

Sweden has worked hard to eradicate its class system over the past 70 years. The original four divisions of nobility, clergy, merchants and peasants began to disappear at the end of the 18th century and were long gone by the turn of the 20th century. The rise of the middle class gave way to the three-class system that exists today. The first, the upper class, includes the few people who have money, influence and power in Sweden. They may have inherited wealth or have acquired it themselves. The third class includes those who do not fit into society, such as criminals or drug addicts. This is also a small class. The middle class, with by far the vast majority of Swedes, includes everyone else. This means that the majority of Swedes have more or less equal status and, in turn, often more or less equal buying power.

As mentioned above, many of the professions in Sweden are accorded equal respect, and through the progressive taxation system, many workers receive similar pay packets each month, and both of these have contributed to the large middle class.

Another factor is the lack of infrastructure for an upper class. Unlike many other countries, there are very few private schools or clubs, and having servants, or even a weekly cleaner is not at all common. Swedes expect to do their work for themselves, and the idea of asking someone else to do their dirty work for them is abhorrent. There is also an informality in everyday life which means that titles, such as Mr. or Mrs. (or Sir or Lady!) are rarely used, and that people prefer to use first names.

However, in the past ten years there has been a subtle shift to the right, and Sweden has seen the biggest growth in the division between wealthy and poor of any country except New Zealand (although it should be noted that these two countries still have among the smallest divisions in the world). Whether this will lead to greater class divisions again has yet to be seen, but most Swedes value the egalitarian society they have shaped over the past century too much to return to the old ways.

The Royal Family

One remnant of the old ways which still remains is the royal family. The present king, Carl XVI Gustaf, and his queen, Silvia, are popular enough to withstand any occasional talk of republicanism. The king is officially the head of state, but holds no political power. He succeeded his grandfather to the throne in 1973, when he was only 27, because his father had died when he was still a baby. In 1976 he married Silvia Renate Sommerlath, a half German, half Brazilian beauty who is loved by the Swedish people for her adoption of Swedish customs and the language. At her 50th birthday celebrations in December 1993 one of the tributes paid to her was that, "sometimes our sleepy country needs a breath of fresh foreign air to wake us up" – and she was that for Sweden.

The crown princess, Victoria, who will accede to the throne after her father (the heir is the first born child, not the first born son in Sweden), was born in 1977; her brother Carl Philip in 1979 and sister Madeleine in 1982. The motto adopted by the king is *För Sverige i tiden* (For Sweden with the times), which is typical of the modern outlook of this monarch. His grandfather, who is often called 'The Old King' because he reigned for so long and became so old, had the motto *Plikten framför allt* (Duty above all), typical of his own time.

The goal of abolishing the monarchy and becoming a republic has been part of the Social Democrats manifesto for years, but as it is not considered to be an important issue it is more or less ignored. The royals are much loved and do a lot of work for Sweden overseas and they are nowhere near as expensive as royals in many other European countries.

MEN AND WOMEN

Sexual discrimination in Sweden is illegal; over 80% of Swedish women work outside the home and 48% of the labour market is female. Women can be ordained priests in the Church of Sweden and the Equal Opportunity Act of 1980 ensures that employers must take active steps to promote equality in the workplace. Sweden has done a lot, particularly in recent years, to work towards equal rights for men and women.

Family Relations

This extends as well to family relations. For example, spouses are taxed separately so that there is no tax advantage either way. Because it is very common for men and women to live together without being married, a law was enacted to protect their rights, called *sambolagen*. *Sambo* comes from *samboende*, or living together, and it is common to refer to a live-in partner as a *sambo*. *Sambo* law means that all belongings of a *sambo* couple are owned equally and must be divided equally if the couple separate. To get this kind of protection in most other countries the couple would have to draw up a special contract; in Sweden couples sometimes draw up their own contracts anyhow, but the law protects them if they do not.

Equality has been furthered also through sharing of childcare. Everyone is entitled to up to a year's paid leave from work to care for a new baby, and that can be shared equally between the father and the mother if wished. Assisted childcare places, time off when a child is ill and state sponsored after-school homes all make it easier for women to advance professionally.

Swedish women still complain that men do not help out enough around the home, and that while they get help with childcare, they are responsible for it, not their partners. In comparison with many other nations, however, Swedes are 'new men' indeed, and it is a rare one who will not share at least partly in housework or childcare.

Unfortunately, despite the initiatives, Swedish women still earn less on average than men, and many of them work part time while their children are small. More men go into higher paid sectors, while women are concentrated in health care, education and service sectors, which tend to be lower paid. This does not seem set to change in the near future. In 1994, although 56% of university students were women, 80% of those studying technical subjects and 63% of those studying science subjects were men. Because parental leave is paid at a percentage of one's salary, the majority of Swedish fathers take only three months or fewer, so that their pay is not affected while their lower paid partner takes often over a year's leave for childcare.

Of course, many women would prefer to stay at home for longer with their children, but few families can afford to maintain their lifestyles without two salaries. The 'superwoman' myth of being able to raise children (albeit with much help), have a demanding and successful career and still keep a beautiful house is as prevalent (and as impossible) in Sweden as it is in other cultures.

The battle for equality between men and women is an ongoing one, but has come much further in Sweden than in most other countries. This may take some getting used to for you, or you may herald it as a wonderful thing but you will certainly notice it.

RELIGION

In spite of celebrating all the religious holidays in the Christian year, and of their history of Christianity, few Swedes are religious any longer. Until recently a Swede became a member of the Church of Sweden automatically on birth, going back to the days when the Church kept census records. If you didn't want to be a member, you could opt out, which would mean you could save 70% of the Church tax which would otherwise be added to your local tax bill. Now no one automatically becomes a member, but can opt to join the Church at the age of 18 if they like.

In fact few opt out and 92% of Swedes are members of the Church of Sweden, even though only 5% are regular church goers. More will also go to the popular services, such as *julottan*, the early morning service on Christmas Day. Sweden today is more of a secular society than a spiritual one. Nevertheless, most children are baptised, with a small family party afterwards, most weddings are celebrated in churches and most funerals take place either in a church or in a funeral with a religious service. Many children choose to be confirmed at about the age of 14, and are prepared for this either through regular classes and attendance at a local church or else through a confirmation camp. The camps are intensive, live-in courses before confirmation, sometimes abroad.

Religious Morality

Many of the morals of the Church of Sweden have been incorporated into the Swedish psyche. The Lutheran doctrine, adopted under Gustav Vasa, preaches submission to the powers that be – and Swedes today are still very obedient to authority. It also endorses diligence in one's duties, another common practice amongst Swedes today. Slacking off or shirking one's duties is seen as sinful, and while Swedes today might not use the word sinful, the belief holds sway in their minds.

Some morals have inevitably been relaxed. It is no longer considered at all sinful to live together before marriage (or even without planning marriage), and more couples have children out of wedlock than married couples. It is not uncommon to have a wedding and baptism ceremony combined, or to have a daughter as flower girl at her parents' wedding. There is a story that this originated long before the current liberal climate and that in rural areas in the past a couple was allowed to sleep together after their engagement. This meant that a combined wedding and baptism ceremony would not have been unusual even then.

The Swedish attitude to marriage and living together is now that they are similar commitments. When a Swedish couple does get engaged they both receive a gold band, which they wear on the ring finger of their left hands. When they marry, the woman often receives a second gold band or a ring with a stone. Getting engaged is not a signal for planning a wedding – many wait 5, 10 or even 20 years before deciding to marry. In the past few years, however, marriage has gained in popularity, though living together is still very common.

Attitudes to homosexual and lesbian relationships are more liberal in Sweden than in many countries. Single sex couples can marry and adopt children, subject to the same application procedure as heterosexual couples. Unmarried single-sex partners enjoy the same legal rights as heterosexual couples (these are the same in any case for married and unmarried couples).

Religious Denominations

Although most Swedes are Lutherans, and religious education is taught as part of the school curriculum, there has been freedom of religion officially since 1951 and unofficially for several centuries before that. This means that all citizens are free to practice their religion, or to choose not to practice a religion at all. The largest non-Lutheran group is that of the Pentecostal Movement, which has over 100,000 members and has gained in popularity recently. Many public figures and media stars have publicly joined, and the members tend to practise their religion more actively than most Swedes do.

Others amongst the ethnically Swedish population include around 140,000 Roman Catholics and 16,000 Jews. The numbers of both of these groups were boosted during and immediately after World War II, but Catholics and Jews have been entitled to worship openly in Sweden since the 1780s and there are established communities of both. The largest congregations of both are in Stockholm, Göteborg and Malmö, and there are religious schools for both in Stockholm and Göteborg, and also a Jewish school in Malmö.

Because of immigration from other parts of the world there are also over 50,000 Muslims, as well as members of Orthodox Churches, Hindus, Buddhists, and members of other Protestant denominations represented in Sweden. All religions other than the Church of Sweden, which is financed through the Church tax, can obtain state grants in proportion to their membership and activities.

If you want to find out about churches, temples or mosques in your area you can check a guide called *Religionsguiden*, available from the

State Immigrant Board (SIV, in Swedish) or from the Immigrant Service Bureau *(Invandrarbyrån)* in your area.

THE SAAMI

The Saami are the indigenous people of Scandinavia. According to Sametinget there are approximately 85,000 Sami across the five northern countries, with about 20,000 in Sweden. (See www.sametinget.se for more information.) In English they are some-times called Lapps, but the name they call themselves, and the preferred name, is Saami *(Samerna* in Swedish).

They are thought to have come to northern Scandinavia about 9,000 years ago, as nomads, and their way of life stayed the same for centuries, until recent years. They lived off hunting, trapping and fishing, and ate mostly reindeer, beaver and salmon. They also traded in furs and crafts, and were reindeer breeders, herding their reindeer across the north with little thought of borders. Their history and religion has very little in common with that of Sweden as a whole, and few would identify themselves as Swedish.

Their language is Finno-Ugric, and has nothing in common with Swedish, which is an Indo European language with Germanic roots. There are three main branches of the language and nine dialects, and it reflects their way of life. For example, there are eight different words for the seasons, as they have the four that we do, plus four more in between those. They are also said to have hundreds of words for snow, and their language can describe an individual reindeer from amongst a herd of hundreds. In recent years their written language and literature has begun to develop, and Saami children can go to Saami language preschools, and their culture and history is taught in schools which teach in both Swedish and the Saami language.

In the past century, problems have arisen for the Saami because the lands they inhabit and use for their herding and hunting have been found to harbour great mineral wealth. The great rivers of the north have often been dammed for hydroelectricity and the growth of the

61

forestry industry has increased industrial interest in the north. Stricter national borders have sometimes made it more difficult for the Saami to cross to different parts of their land. Many younger Saami have given up the old ways of life and moved to Stockholm to live as modern Swedes.

Only about 10% of Saami today are full time reindeer breeders and their methods have changed markedly. They use snowmobiles, mobile phones and helicopters to help in their work, although they prefer to live otherwise as they have always done. This, ironically, leads to some conflict with the burgeoning tourist trade in the region, who want to see picturesque scenes of old Saami customs without the modern trappings.

To help combat these problems, the Nordic Saami Council was formed in 1986, and a flag created for the Saami people. The Saami who live in Sweden have had their own parliament since 1993. Unfortunately the Saami were forced to take this development with a grain of salt; on August 25, 1993, the day before the parliament was formed, the Swedish government abolished hunting restrictions for non-Saami in mountain regions. Many Saami felt that the government had given with one hand and taken with another. Trying to come to terms with the modern and the traditional is an ongoing issue in Sweden.

THE NEWEST SWEDES

After the great emigration in the last century, Sweden has seen much immigration this century, and many of these newest Swedes have settled into Sweden, changing the country slightly and assimilating themselves. About a million people in Sweden today are reckoned to be immigrants, but that includes anyone born to an immigrant, even if their other parent is Swedish and they themselves were born in Sweden. The majority of all immigrants come from other Nordic countries.

The first great wave started during the 1930s and 1940s, when

The first great wave started during the 1930s and 1940s, when Finnish children were evacuated from the War and as many as 30,000 refugees from the Baltic countries sought shelter. Many also escaped the German occupation in Denmark and Norway to settle in Sweden.

After the War, Swedish industry was booming and had a shortage of workers. Representatives of Swedish companies recruited workers from many countries, and many came from Germany, Italy, Greece, Austria, Belgium and the former Yugoslavia. When they arrived in the 1950s and 1960s they were welcomed – the labour was badly needed.

At that time Sweden also welcomed many refugees. From 1950–1973 around 25,000 Eastern Europeans fled to Sweden, particularly from Hungary in 1956, Czechoslovakia in 1968, and Poland in the 1960s. From 1967–1974 about 10,000 Greeks were granted asylum in Sweden, as were around 800 Americans, who refused to fight in the Vietnam War and applied to Sweden for asylum. Various international disasters and tragedies have led to an influx from different parts, including about 1,000 Ugandans in the 1970s, 12,000 Assyrians and Syrians in 1967 and beyond, 11,000 from Latin America, and 2,000 from Vietnam.

All of these refugees have been welcomed and offered assistance in settling into Swedish life. In recent years the refugees have come from Eritrea, Somalia, Ethiopia, Iran, Iraq, Turkey and the former Yugoslavia, and their welcome has not been so hearty. The government has cut down on the number of refugees Sweden can afford to accept, and there has been some anti-refugee, anti-immigrant feeling amongst some Swedes. The majority of Swedes are proud that they are able to share a safe haven with people in need, but sometimes wonder how it is all to be financed. Remember that Swedes need a high level of security, and anything which might threaten that worries them. It is always easier for a nation to welcome immigrants and refugees when the economy is strong.

market remained and remains open, but it is increasingly difficult to immigrate to Sweden unless one has a family or business connection. Currently just over a million immigrants live in Sweden, of which about a third come from Europe (outside Scandinavia), just over a quarter come from other Nordic countries and most of the rest come from Asia (including Turkey). Although nearly 11% of inhabitants are foreign-born, almost half of those have become Swedish citizens.

Swedish society prefers harmonious assimilation from its immigrants, and many immigrants do just that. There are many immigrant support groups both for specific nationalities and for immigrants in general which help people to keep their cultures intact while living as Swedes. All immigrants are protected by legislation against discrimination on the grounds of race, ethnicity or nationality. This legislation also says that immigrants have the right to equality, freedom of choice and cooperation from Swedes. After two years of living in Sweden immigrants can vote in local elections.

Immigration from non-Nordic countries is very gradually changing the face of Sweden, and the newest Swedes are making a subtle and often much welcomed mark on the country, from their small businesses to their contributions to the national sports teams and the arts.

— Chapter Four —

SVERIGE ÄR FANTASTISK!

"… our land is big enough for the one who has a mind and spirit great enough to fill the empty expanses, and with great thoughts to populate the empty wilderness …"

—from Strindberg's *Gustav Adolf*

THE LOVE OF NATURE

Ask a Swede what he or she loves about Sweden and the most common answer will be *naturen* — the nature, or countryside. They love the land itself, not just the freedom, the political system most think is the only way, the language and their homes, but the wide open spaces, the lakes and seashores and great forests. Swedes love their country in a way that some other nationalities may not understand, and it's not unusual to hear them say *"Sverige är fantastisk!"* (Sweden is fantastic – an easy translation from English).

65

Even the national anthem celebrates the beauty of the land, with no mention of royal families and only a brief (and somewhat vague) reference to past and future glories, unlike most other national anthems. The melody comes from a Västmanland folk song, and the lyrics were written in the 19th century by Richard Dybeck. Here they are (in Swedish, of course!)

> *Du gamla, du fria, du fjällhöga Nord*
> *du tysta, du glädjerika sköna.*
> *Jag hälsar dig, vänaste land uppå jord*
> *din sol, din himmel, dina ängder gröna*
> *din sol, din himmel, dina ängder gröna*
>
> *Du tronar på minnen från fornstora dar*
> *då ärat ditt namn flög över jorden.*
> *Jag vet, att du är och du blir, vad du var*
> *Ja, jag vill leva, jag vill dö i Norden*
> *Ja, jag vill leva, jag vill dö i Norden*

The anthem salutes the old, free and mountainous north, with its solitude and beauty; it salutes the best country on earth, especially its sun, sky and green fields; and finally, it salutes Sweden's glorious past. The end refrain expresses the desire of Swedes to live and die in the north.

Flying the Flag

The Swedish flag is often to be seen flying in front of schools, town halls and private homes. There are sixteen national flag days, when all flags should be flown, and many local flag days when flags in just one city or county are flown. Families usually also fly the flags when they are celebrating a birthday or wedding or special day. Even Swedes who do not seem particularly nationalist love their flag, and at major sports events Swedes will paint their faces and dress entirely in blue and yellow to support the Swedish team or athlete. The flag, a yellow cross on a blue field, is the symbol of Swedish freedom.

The writer August Strindberg felt that the national colours ought to be red and green, to symbolise the red paint on the traditional Swedish wooden house, on a background of green fields and trees, and it is true that you see this colour combination everywhere. One of the most beautiful aspects of Sweden, for both natives, immigrants and tourists alike, is the way one can be in unspoiled countryside so near to the cities. Although this is mostly because of the small population density, Sweden realised early how precious its countryside was, and protected a lot of its land in the form of national parks and other protected areas. As much as 3.5% of the country is protected in some way – and much of the rest of it is unspoilt and unpopulated.

Environmental Protection

There are five different ways of formally protecting land. The first, the national parks system, is perhaps the best known. Land in the parks is protected for both research and recreational purposes. The biggest parks are in the far north, and when three of them, Stora Sjöfallet, Sarek and Padjelanta, are put together, they form Europe's biggest wilderness, at 5,330 square kilometres (2,132 square miles). Other parks include Abisko in the north, Skuluskogan, Sonfjället and Hamra in central Sweden and Gotska Sandön, Norra Kvill, Store Mosse and Blå Jungfrun in the south. There are 19 in total.

Nature reserves protect areas which are characteristic of Swedish nature, or have a strong meaning for it, while nature conservation areas are similar but smaller. Slightly different are *Djurskyddsområde* which protect areas for the animals which live there. These are most common for birds, seals and beavers. Finally, there are *Naturminne*, or nature reminders, formed in order to protect the knowledge of the land's nature, beauty or its remarkable quality.

In this way Sweden is working to preserve its beautiful countryside for all to enjoy. Among the animals native to Sweden are wolves, foxes, reindeer, lemmings, bears, moose, lynx, grouse, golden eagles and many other northern birds and mammals. About 60 types of mammal, 230 types of bird, 160 types of fish and 18 types of reptiles, amphibians and related animals make their homes in Sweden.

EVERY MAN'S RIGHT

If you enjoy walking, hiking or camping in the countryside, Sweden will be a wonderful destination for you. Even if you are not near any of the national parks, you can enjoy walking on open land because of the Swedish tradition of *Allemänsrätten* – 'every man's right.' This allows everyone to enjoy the countryside, even if the land is private, within certain rules. Walking in fields and forests, picking flowers, berries and mushrooms, and swimming and boating in lakes and the sea are all considered rights for everyone who lives in Sweden. It is important, however, to remember your obligations towards the land (and the people who may own it), so try to keep in mind the following rules when you venture out into the countryside.

Photo: Robert Grahm

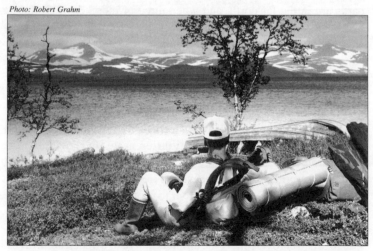

'Every man's right' means that Swedes are entitled to enjoy the countryside, as long as no damage is done. Here a Swede takes a break from walking on a trail in northern Sweden.

Crossing Other People's Land

As long as you do not damage growing crops or seedlings, and do not trespass in someone else's private garden (the land immediately surrounding a private house), you can walk or ski on other people's land without having to seek permission from the owner of the property. If the land is fenced in you can still go across, as long as you shut the gate properly behind you and do not damage the fencing. It is illegal to climb over any fence enclosing a private home.

There are certain exceptions to this rule. The military will restrict access to some areas for defence reasons, and you are not allowed to disturb any areas which are set aside for the protection of animals. These areas will be signposted. Any signs forbidding entry can only be put up with the permission of the local authority (except, again, for the land immediately surrounding a house).

Camping

You may put up a tent and camp for a night or so if the land is not near a private house and is not being used for farming or cultivation of crops, and you don't need to ask the landowner's permission. For longer than a day, or if you are near a private house at all, you should ask permission, but few will refuse you unless you are likely to damage something. This is only for one tent – any groups who want to camp should always ask for permission.

Boating and Swimming

You are allowed to swim and also to moor your boat temporarily and go ashore at any point except at a private house or where the area is restricted for military purposes or to protect wildlife. You can row, sail, canoe, or drive a motor boat in water which belongs to other people, but there may be special restrictions (such as speed limits or a ban on water-skiing).

Picking Berries and Plants

You may pick wild berries, flowers and mushrooms, and pick up fallen branches and dry wood. Some plants are protected because of their rarity, and you are not allowed to pick these (check with your local authority if you are not sure), nor are you allowed to take growing trees or bushes, bark, leaves, acorns, nuts or resin from growing trees. This is because it will damage the trees, and is considered to be theft.

Taking a bird's nest or eggs is absolutely forbidden, and there is no 'every man's right' to hunt.

Making Fires

As long as you are sure that it is safe to do so, you are allowed to light a fire. It must be completely extinguished before you move on, and in certain areas can be banned during times of drought. Fires are not allowed to be built on rockcliffs, as they might crack.

Taking Dogs Out in the Countryside

You can walk your dog freely in the countryside, but during the spring and the summer (between March 1 and August 20) you must keep it on a lead. At all times you need to make sure your dog is under control so that it won't scare or hurt any wildlife.

Clearing Up After Yourself

Anytime you have been out walking, boating, camping or otherwise enjoying the countryside, you must tidy up after yourself. This is simply good manners; do not leave rubbish lying about. You should not leave rubbish bags beside a rubbish bin when the bin is full because animals can easily tear them open and spread the rubbish around. It's easy for animals to injure themselves on cans, bottles, plastic bags or other pieces of rubbish.

The rules of 'every man's right' exist only to protect the land from any careless or foolish damage, and the rules come from basic common sense. Such a privilege carries responsibilities with it, and you must not abuse it.

THE GREEN MOVEMENT

Swedes feel this way about nature overall, which explains why so many are environmentally conscious. They recognise the need to leave the land as undamaged as possible for their children and grandchildren to enjoy, and the government encourages environmentalism through support for recycling, responsible farming and careful labelling of consumer goods.

Recycling and Reusing

You will notice some of these green initiatives right away, because of the prevalence of recycling. Swedes recycle cans and bottles in supermarkets and food shops, where special machines pay them back their deposit in return for the bottle or can. Similar in concept to the American 'bottle bill,' the machines make it easier and more convenient to operate. In most residential and business areas you will see large tips for collecting newspapers and glass that does not carry a deposit on it, and small bins for batteries. You must dispose of certain liquids, such as oil and paint, by giving them in at petrol stations. Some parts of these are also recycled.

Perhaps because Swedes are only a few generations removed from a rural society, there is also a trend towards saving things (such as glass jars to be used as jam jars, for example), or selling them secondhand (often through the columns of the Sunday newspapers) or else donating them to churches or sports groups who will sell them in second hand shops to raise money. They have a tendency to refurbish and repair possessions rather than simply buy new items – partly again because of their history, and partly because material possessions are not as cheap in Sweden as in some other Western countries.

Other environmental initiatives include encouraging consumers to choose less damaging detergents and cleaning materials, and to buy more goods, such as toilet rolls, paper and stationery, made from recycled items.

One new arrival in Sweden found out that many Swedes disapprove of non-environmental cleaning when she asked her new neighbour what the Swedish word for bleach was, so that she could buy it to clean her toilet. Her neighbour told her, "You don't use bleach to clean in Sweden, it's far too strong and harms the environment!" You can use bleach, and there are Swedes who do, but the neighbour wanted to discourage the new arrival from doing so. (By the way, the word is *chlorin*, and it's widely available, though not used as much in daily cleaning as it is in many other countries.)

Farming Methods

The differences in Swedish agriculture because of the effects of environmentalism may not be immediately obvious to you, but you may like to know that Swedish farmers work to keep their farms as natural as possible. This means that when you buy a chicken in a shop it may not look on the surface as large and succulent as the chicken you are used to, because Swedish chickens are not fed with artificial hormones to encourage growth.

You may notice the difference in the taste of milk – called 'Swedish milk from the open countryside' – because the cows are not kept cooped up and fed hormones. The cruel treatment of veal calves and of any other farm (or domestic animal) is illegal.

This doesn't mean that Sweden is a haven of environmentalism, and that there is no pollution or abuse of the countryside. What it does mean is that Sweden works to protect its natural assets, and that the need for environmental initiatives is widely accepted. In fact the milk sold at McDonald's in Sweden is organic as are the meals you can buy at train-stations. To buy organic food in Sweden look for the KRAV mark, which certifies the food. You can find out more about their certification process at www.krav.se.

THE OUTDOORS LIFE

Many favourite pastimes in Sweden centre around nature and the countryside. When I asked eight separate classes of English language students what they liked to do best on the weekends, the most common response was, "Go for a walk in the woods." Some of the other responses were very similar, such as jogging in the woods, berry or mushroom picking, or picnicking out in the country.

You can enjoy any of these pastimes on your own, or you may like to join one of the excursions and rambles organised by a local association or by the town's own recreation committee (*fritidsnämnden*). These committees are charged with ensuring that all who live in the town have an opportunity to enjoy outdoor (or indoor) recreation, and they work with many recreation centres and associations. Several such associations have united in the Swedish Guide and Scout Council (www.scout.se/eng/), and over 140,000 Swedish children join to camp and enjoy many other outdoor activities with them. Another organisation, for all ages, is *Friluftsfrämjandet* (open air supporters' group), which offers open air schools for children and teenagers, and training courses for recreation leaders.

Many towns and cities have marked trails, suitable for walking, running, and skiing, and sometimes also for cycling and horseback riding – details are often given in the local phone books. Many adult education centres offer courses in recognising edible mushrooms, so you can learn to enjoy fresh mushrooms safely. Other popular outdoor pursuits include gardening, camping and outdoor sports. Even aerobics turns into an outdoor sport in Sweden in the summer, with instructors setting up on platforms with boom boxes in the public parks.

Roughing It?

Under 'every man's right,' you can pitch one tent and spend a night anywhere without asking permission, but for many Swedes camping is a fine art, supported by cars full of equipment and an extensive network of campgrounds. Many of these campgrounds have electricity hook-ups for caravans and a separate area for tents, and provide not only hot showers, toilet blocks, barbecues, picnic tables and a local emergency shop, but added extras such as washing machines and dryers, television rooms, mini-golf, tennis, boat hire and cafes. If you don't want to sleep in a tent or a caravan you can rent a small cabin with running water and bunkbeds in many campgrounds. The idea behind all of these places is that you need a place to sleep and store your gear, but otherwise you will want to enjoy the fresh air for meals and all your recreation. Some of the campgrounds stay open all winter long – camping in the snow is not that unusual although the cabins will rarely be heated.

Hiking and Walking

These are popular pastimes throughout Sweden although the most challenging routes are in the northern national parks, especially Sarek, where only very experienced hikers should go, ideally with a guide. There are many Swedish Tourist Foundation (STF) huts along routes, and you can stay a night there for a small fee. It's worth getting in touch with STF if you are interested in doing any hiking, as they can provide a lot of useful information on routes, places to stay and guided tours.

Fishing

With over 96,000 lakes and a long coastline, fishing has always been popular in Sweden. Grilling your own freshly caught fish in the open air on a sunny Swedish evening will certainly help you appreciate the native love of the countryside. For most fishing you will need to buy a fishing permit, although the coastline and some parts of Vänern, Vättern, Mälaren and other large lakes are considered to be open water. Note that many permits only cover fishing with a rod and reel, not with a net, and that fishing off of a boat is sometimes restricted.

Domänfiske is one authority which administers over 1,000 lakes and rivers and sells inexpensive permits for its own areas. You can buy these annually, weekly or daily. They publish brochures with more information, available directly from Domänfiske, on 021 19443, or via their website, www.sveaskog.se, which also offers information on hunting. Contact your local tourist office or authority for informa tion on any open water in your area. If you have lived in Sweden for fewer than two years you should contact the police or the National Board of Fisheries *(Fiskeristyrelsen)* in Göteborg for a special permit for foreigners (not needed for citizens of Scandinavian countries).

Hunting

Hunting is even more restricted than fishing, but remains popular amongst many Swedes, particularly in the middle to northern region. You must own or lease land with hunting rights, and only hunt animals during their specific seasons. A hunting schedule *(jakttabell)* is published every year which gives details of the opening and closing days of a season for each animal. If an animal is not included in the *jakttabell* it is always illegal to hunt it. You can buy the schedule at most gunsmiths, sports shops and ironmongers/hardware stores. Note that if you want to buy (or own) a gun you must apply for a gun licence from the police; gun ownership is strictly controlled.

Skiing

Both cross-country and downhill skiing are extremely popular in Sweden, with excellent mountain resorts in the north and along the Norwegian border. Not many of these resorts are visited by non-Swedes – the Norwegian resorts are if anything better, and other Europeans travel to the Alps – but they are packed with school, work and family groups throughout the winter. Parts of southern Sweden see very little snow, particularly on the coast, so skiers travel even for cross-country trails. If you don't ski when you move to Sweden, you should certainly try it; it's one of the best ways to enjoy the coldest times of the year and, of course, it's outdoors. You can often borrow equipment from friends, otherwise you will certainly be able to rent it at any resort.

For safety's sake, note that some mountainous areas are susceptible to avalanches *(lavin)* – they are marked with yellow signs showing buried skiers. The risk is greater on steeper slopes, in new snow, in high winds and rising temperatures. Stick to the marked trails to be safer. Even if you are an experienced cross-country skiier, you should not leave the marked trails without a good map and equipment, and do check the daily forecast before you set out. Whether skiing or hiking, you should always make sure someone knows that you are going, and leave a copy of your route so that rescuers, if necessary, will know where to look for you.

If you enjoy watching skiing, make your way to Mora for the Vasaloppet, the 86 kilometre cross-country ski race commemorating Gustav Vasa's flight in 1523, which attracts thousands of participants. You can also enter if you enjoy a challenge but remember it takes even the fastest up to four hours to complete. World Cup skiing is widely covered on Swedish television.

Boating

Sailing is one of Sweden's most popular sports, whether on the west coast, in the Stockholm archipelago or on the thousands of lakes. You can take sailing lessons or join a sailing club in many coastal towns, and many children enjoy messing about in dinghies during the warm summer months. If you already sail it's worth meeting up with other sailors just to learn the Swedish sailing terminology, especially if you enjoy racing; many clubs organise weekly competitions. Canoeing, rowing (both rowboats and racing shells) and motorboating are also popular, with kayaking a growing sport. Canal boats ply the Göta Canal from Göteborg to Stockholm in the summer.

If you plan to cruise around Sweden you should buy the STF's annual *Båtturist* book, which gives details of 460 guest harbours, as well as facilities, prices, services and radio details. You'll need a permit from Televerket if you want to operate a VHF radio. The normal boat safety channel is 27.095 mHz, and the 90 000 emergency services telephone number covers the sea rescue network as well. You can buy charts in many harbour sailing shops, or ask at tourist offices.

With thousands of lakes and a long coastline, boating is a favourite pastime for many Swedes. These Swedes are journeying to a summer house on one of the Bohuslän islands.

Cycling

Sweden is one of the countries where cycling is still a good alternative to driving, and many Swedes cycle to work or school, even in the winter, on the network of cycle paths. These are generally separated from streets for safety's sake, and the network can take you around the country as well with over 20 off-road and posted national routes, all with extra information available. The longest tour is *Sverigeleden*, which links many of the routes into one over 6,000 kilometres long. Racing, touring and mountain bikes are all popular, and you should be able to find a new or used one within your price range.

Cycle paths information is available from tourist offices, or look up *Cykelfrämjandet*'s website at cykelframjandet.a.se. As not much information is given in English, however, it might be easier to email them at cyklamera@cykelframjandet.a.se. Cycle races are popular, and the longest one is *Vättern Rundan*, a 300-kilometre race around the lake of Vättern in June – again, only for experienced cyclists.

Orienteering

This cross-country race was invented by a Swede in 1918, and includes running a secret route with the help of a map and compass. It is based on military exercises and has become very popular in Sweden, with many meets and competitions staged in different areas throughout the late spring, summer and early autumn. The biggest meet is the five day long *O-Ringen*, in July every year, where thousands compete in different age and ability classes.

Like sailing or skiing, orienteering is a sport in which all family members can enjoy the outdoors and compete in friendly meets.

Other Sports

There are many other ways to enjoy being outside, but perhaps the most popular of all is through more sport. The Swedish Sports Federation reckons that almost half of Sweden's inhabitants are

Swedes enjoy the outdoors, no matter what the weather. The sea moat behind this fort has frozen over – so it's time to take advantage of a new place to skate and play ice-hockey.

members of a sports club, and that two million people actively participate, either playing, coaching or otherwise supporting the club.

Golf, tennis, football, ice-hockey, table tennis and handball are amongst the sports where Swedes have excelled internationally; and whenever a Swedish team or athlete does well abroad, it boosts interest in the sport at home, as Christian Olsson and Kajsa Bergkvist have done for athletics and Anja Persson and Per Elofsson for skiing. As for tennis, Swedish player Thomas Johansson won the Australian Open in 2001.

Swedes follow their national sides devotedly and if you live in Sweden for any length of time you'll have much more to talk about if you can take an interest in their sports heroes. The three greatest heroes of the past are Björn Borg in tennis, Ingmar Stenmark in downhill skiing and Ingemar Johansson in boxing. Nowadays the Swedish football, ice-hockey and handball teams are revered, as well as Pernilla Wiberg in skiing, Patrik Sjöberg in the high jump in athletics and Helen Alfredsson, Lise-Lott Neuman and Annika Sörensten in golf. Swedes cheer on Vladimir Smirnov, from Kazakstan, in cross-country skiing races, as he lives and trains in Sweden.

Sports Clubs and Societies

It is said that when two Swedes meet they start a society, and the over 22,000 sports clubs in Sweden seem to bear this out. The Swedish Sports Confederation holds to the motto of "Youth Sports and Sports for All" and more than 66% of boys and 50% of girls between the ages of 7 and 15 belong to a sports club. These clubs are the foundation of the sports movement in Sweden and rely heavily on the more than 500,000 Swedes who volunteer as leaders. The independent and democratic sports club system is a very special one in Sweden, and underlines the Swedish love of consensus and cooperation.

In addition to the 63 specialised sports federations which make up the Swedish Sports Confederation, there are category federations such as the School Sports Federation, the Association for Company Sports (there are over 18,000 company sports clubs) and the Sports Organisation for the Disabled. According to the Confederation, the aim is to include old, young, able-bodied, disabled, men, women, Swedes, immigrants, carefree keep-fitters and almost fanatically serious elite athletes, and all spectrums between. Some federations are huge – the Swedish Football Association, for example, has 3,200 clubs – while others are much smaller.

If the sport you play is not represented locally, or if you just want to, you can start up your own club. There should be at least ten of you, and you should agree on what sports you want to concentrate on. The local authority can advise you as to where you can meet and train, and whether you are eligible to receive any financial grants. For a sport to actually join the Confederation it must satisfy certain conditions: it must be non-profit; it must accord with the ideology and goals of the moment; it cannot be related to a sport already represented; it must be spread over at least half of the sports districts; and it must have at least 50 member clubs and 3,000 members.

Every student in any Swedish school studies sport and health as a separate subject in primary and secondary schools. In addition, public sports secondary schools, covering 32 sports, allow young athletes to study and train and compete with other young sportsmen and women. The largest such schools train athletes in skiing, athletics, ice-hockey, football, and orienteering. Top sportsmen can choose to do their military service in a special sports platoon. There are nine sports platoons with about 200 recruits who are allowed to spend 25% of their time in training.

SPORTS CALENDAR

The biggest events in the Swedish sport year include competitions both in Sweden and abroad. The purely Swedish ones, however, are special to the Swedish heart. The calendar looks like this:

- **Feb/March:** World Cup Skiing at Lake Siljan.
- **March:** *Vasaloppet*, the cross-country skiing race in Mora.
- **May:** *Göteborgsvarvet*, a half marathon with over 35,000 participants.
- **June:** *Vätternrundan*, the cycling tour around Lake Vättern.
  SEO, the Swedish golf tournament, which moves each year.
  Vansbro, a three kilometre swimming race held in Dalarna.
- **July:** *DN-Galan*, the athletics meet sponsored by Dagens Nyheter.
  Gotland Runt, a sailing race around the island of Gotland.

	Five Day *O-Ringen* in orienteering.
	Båstad Grand Prix tennis tournament.
• August:	Stockholm Marathon.
• August/Sept:	*Finnkampen.* The longest running track and field competition between two nations is in Stockholm and Helsinki on alternate years, and is always sold out.
	Lidingöloppet, a 30 kilometre road race.
• November:	Stockholm Open Tennis.

Anyone can compete in many of these events (except the elite competitions, such as World Cup skiing, *Finnkampen* and the golf and tennis events) but thousands watch them as well. If you can complete the *Vasaloppet, Vätternrundan, Vansbro* and *Lidingöloppet* in the same year you have achieved a *Klassikern.* Amazingly, more people accomplish this every year.

O-Ringen – the largest orienteering competition – attracts thousands of entrants every July. Many participants and spectators gather here around the finish line.

IN THE SUMMER AND IN THE WINTER

Swedes take it easy in the summer, enjoying the outdoors and sports, and often retiring to small cottages by the sea, in the mountains or near lakes, where they can relax and forget about modern life.

In the winter it's another story, and while many sports are enjoyed year round, or even in winter only, Swedes have many other hobbies to take them through the long dark months. Aside from cultural pursuits, which we will look at in Chapter Eight, many Swedes enjoy creating and fixing things to make their lives more pleasant and comfortable. Knitting and embroidery are popular, as are woodworking and painting. Swedes love to work on their homes, and practice DIY *(gör det själv)* on everything from car repairs to home improvements. Some of the older crafts, such as candle-making, are popular in some areas. Home-baking and sewing are hobbies for some, while others consider them simply a part of everyday life.

Self Improvement and Adult Education

Swedes are fond of self improvement, and what better way to improve oneself than by attending a course? Adult education follows a long tradition of study circles in Sweden, where traditionally a group of people would get together to learn a craft, a language or an academic subject together. The leader is not considered a teacher, but simply further ahead than the others and therefore able to lead them.

Nowadays, formal classes, with a qualified teacher and a certificate at the end are as prevalent as study circles, particularly where the subject can be business related. In a class the teacher will set the pace while the members of a study circle decide themselves how quickly they want to learn and how much work they want to do (consensus again). Most study circles or evening classes meet once a week, in the evenings or on the weekends, and are a good way to get to know other people who share your interests. Subjects such as guitar playing, car maintenance and basketweaving tend to be less expensive than computer programming or navigation.

SWINGLISH OR SVENGELSKA?

DO YOU SPEAK ENGLISH?

Before you move to Sweden everyone will tell you that all Swedes speak wonderful English. Then you move to Sweden and find out that the Swedes who have spoken English abroad speak wonderful English. The Swedes who haven't travelled abroad or have remained silent, don't. They have probably learned it in school (English language instruction has been compulsory for over fifty years) but then, you may have learned French or Spanish in school, and how much of that do you remember?

You can certainly get by in Sweden without learning the language, unlike many other countries, but you will miss a great deal by doing so. Swedish is not a difficult language for an English-speaker to learn, and speaking the language will greatly enhance your time in Sweden. If you hope to work or study in Sweden it is difficult to succeed in either without the language, but even if you just want to socialise with other Swedes they will find it much easier, and you will gain much more insight into the country, if you can converse in Swedish.

Swedish is one of the Indo-European languages, and is Germanic in origin. Swedish-speakers can usually understand some Norwegian and Danish and vice versa. There are about 18 million speakers worldwide, with pockets of them in Finland and Estonia. If you can speak German, Dutch or Afrikaans in addition to English you will find learning Swedish much easier. In fact you may be able to read some basic Swedish even without studying it.

LEARNING SWEDISH

The words 'to teach' and 'to learn' are nearly the same thing in Swedish *(att lära* and *att lära sig)*. One means to teach, and the other to teach oneself, which sums up the Swedish idea of guiding people through learning. If you have an opportunity to learn some Swedish before you come to Sweden you will find it much easier to improve. Several companies, such as Linguaphone, produce book and tape combinations to teach yourself Swedish, or you can sometimes find Swedish lessons if you live near a big city.

Language Courses

However, if you come to Sweden knowing none of the language, you have a few further options. If you are registered and have a residence permit, you have the right to 240 hours of free Swedish language instruction, through the SFI (Swedish for Immigrants) schools, although in some municipalities students may have to pay a small fee towards their books and materials. These courses generally consist of four 45-minute class periods a day, five days a week, with breaks at Christmas, Easter, the summer and whenever the ordinary schools

Once you have applied for a place you will be assigned to a class time and school within your area.

The SFI courses will take you through three stages; the first is basic Swedish, progressing onto more advanced grammar and then to more conversation. You take a test at the end of each level to ensure you can move onto the next one. At the end of the second level you will usually take a test in basic Swedish history and customs. This is to help immigrants assimilate better into Swedish society. If you have not completed the equivalent of the nine years of compulsory schooling that Swedes have you can also have basic classes and more Swedish lessons to bring you up to the same level.

Once you have passed the third level you have completed your SFI schooling – this is often before 240 hours. If you can't pass level three before you have had 240 hours your case will be considered by the school. You will usually be given more time, as long as you have been working and not neglecting your studies. While enrolled in SFI classes you may also be offered extra classes based around hobbies and conducted in Swedish. For example, sewing, guitar, baking or driving lessons are popular. You can practice Swedish in a relaxed environment and learn the specialised vocabulary you need.

It is worth remembering that your rights as an immigrant include the right to paid time off work for Swedish language instruction (through an SFI class). As far as your children are concerned, they have the right to extra Swedish language instruction through the schools to help get them to the same level as their classmates. In addition, they should have extra lessons in their own language, to ensure that they have the best chance of being bilingual. In practice this is difficult to ensure if the child's native language is an unusual one, especially if you are living in a small town or rural area, but the authorities will do their best.

In recent years, because of budget cuts, some native English-speakers have not been able to have extra lessons from *hemspråkslärare*, or native tongue teachers, on the grounds that the children already study English as a foreign language in school and there is already a much greater overall exposure to English than to other immigrant languages. There is also a pilot project now working, to see if English can be taught at a younger age in schools and integrated with other subjects such as foreign history or sciences.

If you do not want, or are not eligible for SFI classes, there are also many evening classes and adult education classes in any number of subjects, including Swedish. Try the Swedish Folk University (*Folkuniversitetet*), or the union-run adult education organisations, such as ABF, TBV or Medborgarskolan. The cost is reasonable and you can choose whichever level and time suits you best.

A final option is either to employ a tutor or to try and pick it up as you go. Some companies will arrange language lessons for their employees and employees' families, as well. If you live with a Swede, try to practice it at home as much as possible – you'll be pleased by how much it helps you.

Finding Fluency

There are said to be at least two stages of learning a foreign language before one is comfortable with it; the first is survival, enabling you to buy a train ticket or ask directions and the second is children's language, which means you will sound like a child grammatically and use a very limited vocabulary. Both of these stages are encouraging. It is when you get beyond these levels that you feel you have reached a plateau impossible to improve on. Your Swedish does not sound any better to you from week to week, and you can understand enough Swedish to hear all of your own mistakes and limitations. Push through this early fluency stage. Others will often hear your improvements, and even if you make lots of grammatical mistakes, they will often be able to understand you. Try to watch Swedish language television, listen to the radio or take out simplified Swedish books (called *lättlästa* or easy reading) from the library – they often have accompanying tapes as well.

THE SWEDISH LANGUAGE

Swedish is of the Indo-European language family, and has Germanic roots, as English does. There are many words which will be familiar to English speakers, such as *man, fisk, hus*, and *rum* which mean, you guessed it, man, fish, house and room. Some words will also be familiar to people from the north of Britain – *barn* (child) in Swedish is similar to the Scottish/North English word 'bairn' for a child. For German speakers the connection is often closer; the Swedish *rådhus* (town hall) sounds almost the same as the German *Rathaus*. Other words such as *billig* (cheap or inexpensive) are the same in both languages.

To make it easier still, Swedish, like English, has borrowed many words from foreign languages. A television is called a TV in Swedish, a pair of jeans is *ett par jeans* and so on. Some words are known in both English and the Swedish translation, such as software (officially *mjukvara*, which is the literal translation of it, but the word software is at least as common). Many of these words start as unwelcome invaders until they are formally adopted by the Swedish Academy. One such recent adoption is the word 'live' when referring to music or a concert. Live music can now be referred to in Swedish as *live musik* and a live concert as *en live konsert*. If you aren't sure of the correct word in Swedish it's often worth chancing an English or German word. Even if it's not correct, the Swede you are speaking with will often understand, and will appreciate you continuing in Swedish – with a one word exception.

The Alphabet

Swedish uses the Roman alphabet, but has 29 letters instead of 26. The last three are *å*, *ä* and *ö*. *Å* is pronounced like 'oa' in boat, *ä* like 'e' in pet and *ö* like 'i' in bird. Remember when you are looking a name up in the telephone book that these are the last three letters in the alphabet, so they won't be next to the ordinary 'A's or 'O's.

In addition, many of the letters are pronounced very differently:

- g sounds like a y before the vowels e, i, y, ä and ö (called soft vowels).

- j, 'dj,' 'gj,' 'hj' and 'lj' also sound like a y before the soft vowels.

- k sounds like a 'ch' before the soft vowels.

- 'sch', 'sj', 'skj', and 'stj' are pronounced differently in the east and west. In the east, they have a strong 'sh' sound. In the west they sound a bit like the sound 'hugh' in English, and it is not an easy sound to learn. Stick with the strong 'sh' if you cannot do it and you will still be understood.

- 'tj' sounds like 'ch.'

A further note about pronunciation: Swedish is one of the few tonal languages in Europe. This means that words which are pronounced nearly the same have different meanings, depending on the tone, or emphasis you give to them. Don't worry about this in the beginning if you are not used to tonality in language, most of the words are so far apart in meaning that you will still be understood through context.

Swedes are often said to sing while they speak. (Listen to Floyd, the Muppet's Swedish chef, singing "Hurdy Gurdy" and you'll understand this.) If you can learn to sing a bit when you speak Swedish you will be understood more easily as well. You may feel like you're mimicking Swedes in a way that might be rude, but in fact you'll be imitating the way they speak their language, one of the best ways to learn a language yourself. English sounds very flat to most Swedes, try not to speak Swedish the same way.

BODY LANGUAGE

Nonverbal language is also important to learn. In general, Swedes do not gesticulate or move around very much when they are speaking, preferring to hold themselves still and rely on the words alone to convey their message. A popular non-word is the sound of people sucking in their breath sharply with a sound almost like 'hup.' This is difficult to describe but you will recognise it when you hear it. It has a multitude of meanings, from: "Okay, now we're finished eating, let's go" to, "What a sad story, what a shame" or perhaps, "Nothing we can do about that I'm afraid" or, "I understand the problem now." When you learn to interject this sound, with sharp breath intakes at the right places, you will really sound Swedish.

There are many other non-word sounds in different accents and areas; you will get used to them as you learn the language. Throughout Sweden they nod their heads to mean yes and shake their heads to mean no.

SWEDISH GRAMMAR

Swedish is one of the easiest languages grammatically for English speakers to learn. The main differences from English are that verbs do not need to agree with their subjects, there are two declensions of nouns and singular and plural forms of 'you' are different.

Verbs, within the present or future or other tense, are the same whether the subject is I/you/he/they and so on. Instead of having to remember: I am/you are/he is, just remember the equivalent of: I are/ you are/he are (in Swedish this is *jag är, du är* and *han är*).

The two declensions of nouns are common and neutral. Eighty percent of nouns are common, and the article for them is *en*. The rest are neutral and their article is *ett*. Another peculiarity is that the definite article comes after the noun rather than before. This means that the word for girl, *flicka*, which is a common noun, becomes *en flicka* (a girl) or *flickan* (the girl) with an article. The same is true in the plural form (*flickor* is girls; *flickorna* the girls). Whether a noun is *en* or *ett* must be learned by rote. Adjectives must also agree with the gender of the noun.

While English has one word for both the singular and plural forms of 'you,' Swedish has two – *du* and *ni*. *Ni* can also be used to be polite to one person, but it is less common than using the equivalents in French or German. Most Swedes will say *du* to one another, even if they have never met before, and it is the common usage.

USEFUL PHRASES

To say yes in Swedish, use *ja*, unless you are answering yes to a negative question, when you should use *jo*. For example, if someone asks you, "Don't you speak English?" and you answer *ja*, they will be confused – do you mean yes, I do speak English or yes, I don't speak English. Use *jo* to mean the first and *nej* to mean the second. Other yes words include *japp* (sounds like the English 'yup') and *javisst* and *jajamen* which mean 'yes, of course' and 'yes, absolutely' respectively. Swedes will often make a noise which sounds like 'aw' to mean yes, or to confirm that they are listening and have understood.

To say hello, say *hej* (hay) which is equivalent to hello. *Hej hej*, equally common, is like 'Hi.' To be more formal you can say *goddag*, *god morgon*, *god afton* or *god natt* which mean good day/morning/ evening/night. Goodbye is generally *hejdå* but can also be *adjö*, taken from the French word *adieu*. It's common to wish someone a good day or good time when leaving, by saying *ha det så bra*, or simply *ha det*. ('have it so good,' shortened to 'have it.')

Courtesies

Thank you is *tack* or sometimes *tackar* or *tack tack*. Swedes do not say the equivalent of 'thank you very much' as much as they say 'thank you,' but if you want to be effusive, say *tack så mycket* ('thanks so much'). There is no Swedish word for please, so just use *tack* again when asking for something. Other options are *snälla* or *vänligen*, both of which mean variants on kind or friendly. The formal expression would be, 'Can you be kind and pass me the butter?' or else, 'Kind Maria, pass me the butter.' In Sweden it is more normal to leave out the 'please' equivalent and merely thank afterwards. Instead of 'you're welcome' or any other English equivalents, say *var så god*. This can also be an invitation for guests to help themselves or sit down. Its literal translation is 'be so good' and the unspoken end of the sentence is what you are being invited to do.

There is no word for sorry, so Swedes will use the equivalents of 'forgive me' *(förlåt mig*, shortened often to *förlåt)* or 'excuse me' *(ursäkta mig*, often shortened to *ursäkta)*. If you want to ask if it's all right to do something, use the expressions, *Går det bra om … ?* (literally, 'does it go well if … ?') or *Gör det något om … ?* ('does it do something if … ?') If you want to switch to English, ask if the person you are speaking with understands English by asking, *Pratar du engelska* or *Talar du engelska*. The Swedish language does not use as many capital letters as English or German, and while proper names and country names start with capital letters, language names and names of days and months do not. A final useful word is *hjälp* (help) which sounds like 'yelp' – close enough to the English word in an emergency.

GREETINGS

Swedes generally shake hands and make eye contact when they greet people. If they have met before, they say *hej*. If they haven't they often simply say their first name by way of introduction. It is at least as common for them to introduce themselves as for their host to formally introduce them. Some Swedes have adopted the European greeting of a single kiss and/or a hug but it is not very common.

Personal space is important to Swedes, and it is not often they will strike up a conversation with a stranger in a train or other public place. If you try it may be welcomed but it may also be seen as threatening. Silence between friends is seen as companionable and not at all worrying. When Swedes do talk amongst friends they do not often interrupt each other, and are not comfortable with interruptions. They tend to speak less overall, and more directly. They rarely gush and like to tell it as it is. Exaggerated expressions common in English (such as 'I love ice-cream' or 'losing that umbrella was tragic') are not often heard in Swedish.

TELEPHONE SWEDISH

Swedes answer the telephone with their names or their telephone numbers, rather than 'hello.' Sometimes this is the whole name, sometimes just the surname. If you telephone and want to speak to someone you should ask, *Kan jag få prata med ...* ('Can I get to speak with ... ?') One answer you may encounter is, *Kan du dröja?* or *Ett ögonblick* ('Can you wait?' or 'Just a minute'). Swedes do not appreciate abruptness on the telephone, and you should always say goodbye before hanging up.

DAYS, DATES, TIME AND NUMBERS

Dates are written backwards for an English speaker. Christmas Day in 1996 is therefore written 961225 officially. You may also see it written as 25/12 1996 informally. Time runs on a twenty-four hour clock, so there is no a.m. or p.m.

To ask the time, say *Vad är klockan?* ('What's the clock?') Half past the hour means half way to the next one, so the Swedish *halv tre* (half three) is really 2:30 in English. It is not uncommon to use the twenty-four hour clock in everyday speech, so that while it is usual to agree to meet at *halv tre*, don't be surprised if someone suggests meeting at 14.30 instead. The abbreviation for the time is *kl.* (For example, the train leaves at kl. 18.00.)

The days of the weeks and the months are very similar to the English words. The week begins on Monday and ends on Sunday, with the Swedish words as follows: *måndag, tisdag, onsdag, torsdag, fredag, lördag* and *söndag*. The months, which, like the days, do not start with a capital letter are: *januari, februari, mars, april, maj, juni, juli, augusti, september, oktober, november, december.* However, they are not usually abbreviated to jan, feb, etc.

When Swedes write numbers, they switch the commas and decimal points that an English-speaker would use. Therefore six thousand Swedish crowns is written SEK6.000, and five and a half percent is written 5,5%.

Useful Abbreviations

• f Kr	*före Kristi*	B.C.
• e Kr	*efter Kristi*	A.D.
• t ex	*till exempel*	for example; e.g.
• osv	*och så vidare*	and so on, etc.
• t o m	*till och med*	until and including
• fr o m	*från och med*	from and including
• bl a	*bland annat*	among others
• ca		circa
• dvs	*det vill säga*	that is to say; i.e.
• f d	*före detta*	previously
• f n	*för närvarande*	presently
• p g a	*på grund av*	on account of
• s k	*så kallad*	so called

All of these abbreviations are commonly written as such, even in the middle of literary works or newspapers. However, in spoken Swedish the full expression is used.

The United Nations is the FN, the European Union the EU, the Olympic Games OS and World Championships are called VM, and all of these abbreviations are used commonly in spoken as well as written Swedish.

OTHER LANGUAGES IN SWEDEN

If you are tired of speaking Swedish, or are only going to be in the country for a short time and don't want to learn the language, in spite of my exhortations to do so, you'll be pleased to know that there is help. As mentioned, English has been a compulsory subject in Swedish schools for over forty years and many Swedes do like to practice their English. You will often find that workers in the post office, banks and shops are very helpful even if their English is a bit rusty.

Accommodating Foreign Languages

One of your rights as an immigrant is to an interpreter when dealing with the authorities. If you need to have an immigration interview it can be conducted in English if necessary. You can also take your driving licence test in English, find an English speaking doctor or health clinic and, in the larger cities, send your children to English speaking schools and attend English speaking religious services.

Swedish libraries provide books and tapes in many foreign languages. In any bookshop there is likely to be a selection of English language books, and many academic books or less popular works are only available in English (the Swedish book-buying market is not large enough to make translations viable for these books). You will usually be able to find British newspapers on sale on the same day in the larger cities and a few days later elsewhere, while North American, Australasian and other newspapers are available in the larger cities a few days after publication. Many specialist magazines do not have equivalents in Swedish and so are on sale in English – or can be ordered by a good newsagent. The government also sponsors a small weekly newspaper of Swedish immigrant news, which is available in all of the main immigrant languages (including English) as well as in simplified Swedish.

Radio and Television

Many of the programmes on Swedish television are bought from overseas, and subtitled rather than dubbed, so you will be able to follow many of the shows familiar to you. Films and videos are also subtitled rather than dubbed, and the newest Hollywood releases are often screened earlier in Sweden than in Britain. Note, however, that children's programmes and films are usually dubbed.

Apart from Swedish television, foreign channels such as BBC Worldwide, Sky, CNN, Eurosport and MTV Europe, as well as various French, German, Danish and Norwegian channels, depending on where you live, are also available if you have a cable connection – most apartment blocks do.

Swedish radio offers specific programming in immigrant languages as well. If you buy a good shortwave radio you will be able to access BBC World Service, Voice of America and various other overseas programmes. Some of the local Swedish stations broadcast news or other programmes in English occasionally – look out for them in the programme schedules in the newspaper.

Immigrant Groups

If you need to speak to someone in your own language, join one of the many immigrant groups which offer help, support, companionship, friendship, volunteer work or a combination of all five. Many long term foreign residents still attend these groups to celebrate national holidays and to keep in touch with their countries. They range from being well organised, with bylaws, statutes and formal connections with the embassy (like the Organisation for American Women) to just an informal group of countrymen who meet occasionally for gossip and to catch up. You can find out about them through the phone book, other local foreigners, your embassy or the social worker *(SYO-konsult)* at the SFI school.

With such a good backup system, you might feel even more inspired to learn Swedish! Although you can manage without it, you will get much more out of the country and enjoy it much more as soon as you learn. In fact the single best piece of advice anyone moving to Sweden can get is to learn at least some of the language, either before you arrive or soon afterwards. Any of the negative things about moving to a foreign country in general, and a cold, northern country like Sweden in particular, will seem minor compared with the positive aspects of learning about a new country when you can understand what is going on.

— Chapter Six —

EATING AND SHOPPING IN SWEDEN

SMÖRGÅSBORD

Anywhere you are in the world, you are likely to have heard of one Swedish meal: the smörgåsbord – especially any Muppets fans, who will be familiar with Floyd, the Swedish chef, and his mutterings of "smorgyborgy." This buffet meal actually means 'sandwich table,' and is nowadays most often found in tourist areas or around Christmas time (when it is called a *julbord*, literally a Christmas table). Plates and plates of different herring and pork dishes, breads, potatoes, salads and cakes are laid out onto a long table for self service. Often the centrepiece is an entire decorated pig's head, and while a buffet is considered to be less formal in many countries, in Sweden an invitation to a smörgåsbord is an honour. It is a delicious meal, but not everyday eating in Sweden.

TRADITIONAL FARE

Now that you are actually going to Sweden, what do the Swedes eat, if not smörgåsbord? The traditional Swedish meals are not unlike those in many northern European countries and are based on potatoes, meat and bread. Not very long ago, most meals consisted of a little meat or fish, a lot of potatoes with some sauce and some bread on the side. Of course, this varied depending on the region. In the north the meat was as likely to be game, whilst on the west coast, fish was eaten much more. The type of bread eaten also depended on the region; the everyday loaf, or *limpa*, seen everywhere now was only eaten in the south, where crops were better.

Swedish crispbread, or *knäckebröd*, comes from the middle regions of Sweden, where the flour could only be ground in the spring and autumn, when there was enough water to drive the mills. Because the flour would not keep for six months, the dry thin crispbread was the obvious answer. The northerners ate *tunnbröd*, or 'thin bread,' which is not unlike a tortilla, because the only crop which would grow there, barley, will not rise and so yeast bread could not be baked. Today all three breads, as well as many other types of loaves, are eaten all over Sweden.

As Sweden was until quite recently a very poor country, most people lived chiefly on herrings and potatoes. When they feasted, however, the pig provided the most popular meats, in hams, bacon, sausages and pork. Although today Swedes eat many different types of food, most of the traditional holiday meals still include meat or fish.

Anyone coming to Sweden from Britain will not be too surprised by the food, but anyone moving from Asia or southern Europe may be rather shocked at the blandness of the food. A lot of the dishes rely on dairy products and sauces rather than spices, and many kinds of food are sweetened. Bread made with sugar in it is something of an acquired taste if you don't have a naturally sweet tooth.

However, if you don't enjoy sweet bread, you can do as many Swedes do and bake it yourself. A lot of Swedes do their own baking, cooking and even gathering of food – it fits in with their enjoyment of the simple life. You can, of course, buy bread and cakes, but most Swedes bake their own. The selection of ready-prepared meals in shops is still not very good (it is getting better as Sweden is now a member of the European Union), and it is less usual for Swedes to rely on prepared foodstuffs such as salad dressing or even jam as they often prefer to make their own.

Fishing, Hunting and Picking

Any country with a long coastline produces lots of anglers and Sweden is no exception. Hunting is also popular in Sweden, and many people enjoy providing their own fish and game for the table (strict laws do regulate this). It is easy for you to join in this even if you don't enjoy fishing or hunting; most Swedes join in the annual pilgrimage to the woods to pick mushrooms and berries all summer and autumn. It is very important, if you have never picked mushrooms before, to go with an expert; some mushrooms are poisonous and while you can (and perhaps ought to) buy a field guide, there are stories every year of enthusiastic mushroom gatherers picking the wrong mushrooms. Most local communities have groups which go on day trips with an expert every weekend in the early autumn, which is an excellent way to learn about the different species. You can also learn different recipes through these groups, and some adult education centres offer evening classes on picking mushrooms.

Berries are less dangerous and probably everyone picks these – even in the cities it is possible to find thickets in the parks. Among the berries you can pick are wild strawberries *(smultron)*, blueberries and lingonberries (a type of cranberry). In the northern half of Sweden you can also find Arctic cloudberries *(hjortonbär)*, a golden berry which makes wonderful jam.

Seafood

Swedes have always eaten a lot of seafood, because it was plentiful and cheap. Now it is less plentiful and cheap, but you will find that many fish and shellfish considered delicacies elsewhere in the world are very common in Sweden. For example, caviar is sold everywhere, and one brand, Kalles Kaviar, which comes in tubes, is very common on Swedish breakfast tables. Better quality caviar, which comes in jars, is often served with toast or as a starter course.

The cheapest fish of all, herring, is now becoming increasingly expensive due to overfishing. However, the *inlagd sill* (herring which is marinated to preserve it) sold in jars everywhere, is still a staple in many Swedish homes. It comes in different sauces, such as mustard, onion and curry, and is perfect with some potatoes, crispbread and salad. As it is eaten raw it may not be to everyone's taste, but it is much better than some of the other 'special' forms of herring beloved to Swedes.

One of the most famous within Sweden is called *surströmming*, which is rotten herring. It is a speciality of the north, and derives from a time when people preserved herring in as little salt as possible (as salt was so expensive), which made the herring ferment. Nowadays it is mostly eaten for tradition's sake, although there are those who claim to enjoy it. Most Swedes who live south of Norrland speak with awe of the dreadful smell which comes out of the tins which the *surströmming* is kept in, and haven't managed to eat it themselves. If you want to try different types of herring (except *surströmming*, which is unusual), the best thing to do is to order a herring plate, or *sillbricka* in a restaurant, or to find a real *smörgåsbord,* where often many different types will be on offer.

Other Swedish favourites include smoked eel, *gravlax* (salmon preserved in salt and dill) and smoked salmon. Indeed, any smoked or preserved fish is still very popular in Sweden.

With all this fish, certain sauces are very popular, including soured cream and *hovmästersås*, a mustard sauce. Dill is often served with herring and with potatoes, and is important in Swedish cooking.

If you are tired of fish, try some game. Reindeer, venison, elk and such birds as grouse are all popular within season, and many restaurants have special game menus during the autumn. These are often served with lingonberry sauce and, of course, potatoes. Occasionally you may find *rotmos*, a mixture of mashed root vegetables, instead of potatoes.

COFFEE AND TEA
Swedes drink the second highest amount of coffee per capita worldwide. They drink it in the morning, after lunch, in the afternoon, after dinner and in the evening. Most Swedes drink it black, and you may like to remind them you take milk or cream if you do – otherwise your cup will be automatically filled up to the rim when you are drinking coffee with friends. Gevalia, a luxury coffee in some countries, is the coffee of choice in Sweden. Nowadays, most Swedes brew their coffee with a filter coffee maker or a cafetiere but older Swedes will still boil up coffee grounds to make a very strong brew. Coffee grounds sold in shops are specially marked if they are for boiling; check that you are buying *bryggkaffe* if you don't want to boil it.

Nowadays more people are starting to drink tea than before, especially herbal teas, which are seen as healthy. Even Swedes who are keen coffee drinkers may drink tea with breakfast and you can certainly find most types in Sweden. Note that if you order it in a restaurant it is likely to be made with a teabag; not a surprise for a North American, but probably best avoided by anyone from a tea-drinking country.

In the big cities in Sweden there are many cafes which serve espresso, cappuccino, cafe au lait or different Brazilian, Kenyan or Tanzanian grinds. Even in smaller towns there will always be a few cafes, or *konditori* where you can order a cup of coffee and a cake.

Having a mid morning or afternoon coffee and cake is a very pleasant custom in Sweden, and there are many cakes, such as cinnamon buns, soft gingercake, sugarcake, *wienerbröd* (Danish pastry) and *mazarin* (Sweden's favourite pastry, an almond tart topped with icing) which are well worth trying. If you like cream you will appreciate Swedish cakes and pastries even more. Most cafes sell cakes to take home as well, and all will sell special cakes in different seasons. You will find saffron buns in early December for Lucia Day, gingersnaps throughout the Christmas season, and *semlor* (rolls filled with marzipan and cream, sometimes served in a bowl of warm milk with cinnamon) between Christmas and Easter.

EATING OUT

If you are out and about and need a snack which isn't sweet, try one of the *gatukök* (literally, street kitchen) about, which traditionally sell hot sausages with bread (like hotdogs) but now are as likely to sell hamburgers and kebabs as well. Even in winter there is usually a queue at these stalls, which move about the streets depending on where the business is. If you are out late you'll see many of them on the streets waiting for the revellers to come out from bars and pubs.

Perhaps, however, you would prefer to eat a proper meal out. Sweden does not have a restaurant culture as many countries do, and it is not usual for Swedes to eat out very often for their evening meal. However, many do eat their midday meal out at restaurants near their place of work, and take advantage of the daily special, which usually includes a hot meal, salad, bread and butter, a soft drink or light beer and the essential coffee for around SEK50 – a bargain in Sweden. Look out for these specials, called *Dagens rätt*; they are an excellent way to eat Swedish meals inexpensively. Note that service is always included, and there is no need to add any extra tip.

Offsetting the Cost

The main reason Swedes do not eat out very often may well be because of the cost, it is certainly not cheap to eat out. If you are in Stockholm, Gothenburg or Malmö it is worthwhile investing in a coupon book called "The Entertainment Book," which offers two for the price of one meals in many restaurants. Ask in any of the hotels about where you can buy one. In general it will pay for itself if you eat out more than twice a year. Each book includes restaurants all over Sweden, but the bulk of them are in one of the three cities, depending on which version of the book you buy.

Not included in the book very often are the local neighbourhood restaurants, called *kvarterskrog*, which are unpretentious even for Sweden. Because Swedes don't eat out very often, it's unlikely that you will meet 'regulars' in there but the restaurants do provide good Swedish home cooking nearby to residential areas, generally at a good price. They are another very good way to try some more traditional Swedish meals

Among the meals you may find served there are:

- Swedish meatballs with lingonberry sauce (made from a combination of pork and beef, although most families have their own recipe).
- *Pytt i Panna*, which is a form of hash, with potatoes and pork fried together.
- *Sjömansbiff*, or 'sailor's beef,' a casserole with beef, onions and potatoes, cooked in beer.

- *Kåldomar* , beef wrapped in cabbage leaves, which is in fact originally a Turkish dish, brought back to Sweden by King Charles XII in the 18th century, and thought of now as typically Swedish.
- Meatloaf.
- Bloodpudding, which is very similar to the Scottish black pudding, a type of blood sausage.
- Rosehip soup *(nyponsoppa)* which is a sweet dessert soup very popular with children.

On Thursdays many Swedes eat pea soup and pancakes (not at the same time, the pancakes are for dessert). Long ago, before the Reformation, Swedes fasted on Fridays, and needed a substantial meal on Thursdays to tide them through. Dried yellow pea soup is extremely filling, and kept them going. Not many people fast on Fridays now, but a great many Swedes eat pea soup every Thursday night still. With mustard it tastes lovely, though it is not easy to get used to drinking the warm *punsch* (a sweet alcoholic drink) with it as the Swedes do.

Another special dish, sometimes served at *kvarterskrog* but more often a holiday dish, is called 'Jansson's Temptation' and is made with herrings, potatoes and onions. It is quite time consuming to make, but delicious, even if you are a bit tired of potatoes at this point.

Although Swedish home cooking or *husmanskost*, is served everywhere, international restaurants are more and more common. Certainly in the cities you will be able to find most types of food, but smaller towns usually have a pizzeria and a Chinese restaurant. Pizzas in Sweden are always served with a shredded cabbage salad, possibly because it was a custom of the first pizzeria owner back in the 1970s.

Sweden does have its fair share of McDonald's, Burger Kings and Pizza Huts as well as Clock Restaurants (a Swedish fast food chain) frequented mostly by younger people. They taste the same here as anywhere else, though the prices may surprise you.

FOOD SHOPPING

When you first start to shop for food in Sweden you may find that the selection is not as wide as it is in your home country – even if you are moving from Britain, which has a similar food tradition. Sweden has long been a homogenous and fairly poor country, and it is only in the past twenty years that immigrants have brought in more exotic foods (spaghetti is still considered exotic to older Swedes).

In the cities there are plenty of shops run by immigrants from Asia, especially China, and the Middle East, where you can find Asian, Middle Eastern and Indian foods, including inexpensive bulk bags of rice and even several types of British foods, like custard. Some smaller towns have these shops; otherwise you may like to make an occasional visit to Stockholm, Gothenburg, Malmö/Lund or Uppsala to stock up. If you have space when you are moving to Sweden it is worth bringing some of the more exotic ingredients you favour – and most foreigners in Sweden do seem to personally import their favourite foods whenever they go home for a visit. With Sweden now in the EU the availability of foreign foods may improve.

Adopting a Local Diet

You may choose to change a lot of what you cook and eat when you live in Sweden, because what you eat at home may not be available, and what most Swedes eat usually is the best use of the less expensive resources. Swedes shop at supermarkets, though in many towns fruit and vegetable stalls are a cheaper option in the warmer months. These stalls are usually run by immigrants, and are a new thing for Sweden; not all towns do have them yet. Near a coastline, however, all towns have fish markets and stalls. Often these move about the town or city and will be in your neighbourhood one morning or afternoon a week (announced in advance). The fishermen occupy these stalls on a rota basis and, while they often can't speak English, they are as helpful as they can be with hand signals and a few words. Once you learn a little

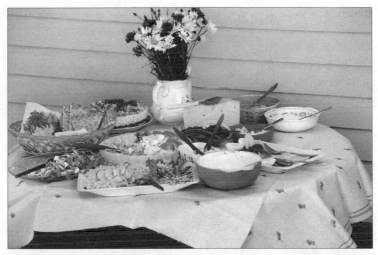

A table set with a typical midsummer buffet. Herring and new potatoes are the main components. Adjusting to a new diet can be difficult but Swedish food is generally healthy and tasty.

of the fish they sell – important if you've never seen some of the North Sea or Baltic varieties before!

In some areas Swedes still shop at many small shops, a baker, a grocer, a butcher, a cheese shop and so on, but the supermarket is popular because it is easy and keeps long opening hours. Shops such as ICA and Konsum are all over Sweden, and are reasonably priced. There are usually a few very low priced shops as well. All supermarkets provide plastic or paper bags, which you have to pay for. Most smaller shops don't, so remember to bring your own. All measurements are in metric, and by law there should always be a *jämförpris*, or comparison price, which allows you to compare prices per 100g on every article.

Systembolaget

A very popular shop in Sweden is called *Systembolaget*, which is the only place that sells alcohol to take away. There are no other wine shops, off-licences, package stores or liquor stores and the state maintains a monopoly on the sale of alcohol.

In general, the most popular alcoholic drink is beer, which in Sweden is usually lager. This comes in four basic strengths; weak (Klass 1 or *lättöl*), which can also be bought in supermarkets and other shops; strong (Klass 3, or *starköl*) and two medium strengths (called *folköl* and *mellanöl*). Usually, *lättöl* is drunk like a soft drink, or if one is driving afterwards. Sweden has extremely strict drink driving laws, so if you are driving you should not order a *starköl*. The strengths of the beers are 1.8%, 2.8%, 3.6% and 4.5%. In Sweden these strengths are a measure of percentage by weight, so the 4.5% strength of a *starköl* is equivalent to 5.4% when measured by volume.

To buy *lättöl* or *folköl* you must be at least 15-years-old. These are not sold in the *Systembolaget* because Swedes don't really consider them to be that alcoholic. To buy anything from the *Systembolaget* (nicknamed just *Systemet*) you need to be 20 years old. There is a definite love-hate relationship between Swedes and the *Systemet*. This has eased in recent years as *Systemet* has increased opening hours (10 a.m. to 6 p.m. weekdays and 10 a.m. 1 p.m. on Saturdays, though some shops have longer hours – see www.systembolaget.se for information about specific shops).

The main office publishes a quarterly guide to the drinks sold in *Systembolagets* nationwide, with prices and with a code number. Most, if not all, shops offer self-service so you can simply pick up what you want, but you can also use the guide to order any of the *Systembolaget's* collection into your local shop.

The assistants receive a lot of training regarding wines and spirits and so if you ask them which wine you ought to serve with poached salmon, they can give you good advice. However, in practice the queues are usually so long that you don't often see people spending more time there than they have to.

Most Swedes like the monopoly because they think the assistants are knowledgeable, and because they believe that the alcoholism problem in Sweden might get much worse if they could buy alcohol anywhere and even on the weekends. The *Systembolaget* monopoly may end in any case, due to pressure from other members of the European Union, but the Swedish government has arranged agreements to keep it as it is until 1997 at least.

Most foreign alcoholic drinks are available in *Systembolagets*, but the prices are frighteningly high. Swedes who travel abroad import their full share of duty-free allowances. Wine and beer are not taxed as heavily as spirits, and they are not much more expensive than in other northern European countries. Drinks such as whisky, vodka and gin are taxed according to their strengths, not their prices, so that the tax on the cheapest blended bourbon will be similar to that on an expensive single malt scotch.

Wine is becoming more popular in Sweden, as most people have travelled abroad and due to the fact that it is now cheaper than before. However, traditionally and at formal parties, Swedes will always drink *snaps* of strong alcohols like *brännvin* and *besk*, which are flavoured shots of pure alcohol. Many Swedes distill these drinks at home, although it is illegal, simply because they have done it for generations. Home brewing of *lättöl* and wine is legal and also very popular.

Other popular drinks you may come across are *punsch*, which bears no resemblance to the English punch, but is instead a strong sweet liqueur made with arrak and drunk very cold with coffee after a meal or, as mentioned above, warm with pea soup on a Thursday evening and *glögg*, which is warm spiced wine served with raisins and almonds at Christmas time.

Alcoholism

A word about alcoholism in Sweden; Swedes are not as used as many other Western cultures to drinking in moderation. They drink very little alcohol on a daily basis but do like to drink a lot when they are out on the town or at a party. Because of this they have earned a reputation in many European resorts of being unable to handle alcohol, and if you see young rowdy Swedes staggering down the street at 3:00 a.m. you may agree.

However, the alcohol problem is not really any worse than in most countries. It is sometimes more noticeable though because it is in such contrast to the general sobriety of the majority of Swedes. There are often a few people queueing outside the *Systembolaget* on a Friday morning (when the benefit money is paid out) and Swedes are very worried about alcoholism. This is why the state monopoly has lasted so long and why many Swedes still support it.

If you go out drinking in the evening with Swedish friends, do not be surprised if they drink more than you would be comfortable with and, whatever you do, don't let yourself be pressured into drinking the kind of *snaps* and spirits that they like! (Unless, of course, you enjoy drinking.) On the other side of the coin, if you are invited to a Swedish home for a casual meal, you are very likely to be offered cider, milk, orange or berry squash or Ramlösa water instead of a beer or wine. Wine and spirits in particular are reserved for parties or special occasions.

MORE SHOPPING

Apart from the necessities of food and drink, when you move to Sweden you are likely to need to buy furnishings for your home and clothing for your family, as well as the consumer items you would normally buy at home. In addition, you will probably want to buy some typical Swedish things as presents or souvenirs of your time in Sweden.

The good news is that Swedes are very internationally-minded consumers and you will be able to find most things in the cities. The bad news is that it is all quite expensive. Value added tax (called *MOMS*) is 25% on most goods in Sweden, although some are taxed at a reduced rate of 12% or 6%, such as books. Food is taxed at only

12% and alcohol taxed at variable rates higher than 25%. You may prefer to buy things when you make visits home or to neighbouring countries. Many Swedes stock up on day or weekend trips to Denmark, Germany, Poland, the Baltic countries and Russia. (Norway and Finland are even more expensive, amazingly). If you are only in Sweden for a short time (and if you are not a European Union citizen), you can receive the MOMS back when you leave the country. Even if you are based in Sweden, you can probably receive the MOMS back if you are buying things to take back home as presents. Most shops will have the 'Tax-free for Tourists' sign in the window, just ask the sales assistant for help with it.

Shopping Hours and Information

Most shops are still open only during the working week, which means 10:00 a.m. to 5:00 p.m. from Monday to Friday and 9:00 a.m. to 1:00 p.m. on Saturdays, though this is often much longer in the bigger cities. In Stockholm and Gothenburg some shops are open on Sundays during the summer tourist season and before Christmas as well. If you are coming from a country with longer opening hours, remind yourself of Swedish hours before you run out of milk at two o'clock on a Saturday afternoon!

Paying by cash is common, but not as common any more as paying with a plastic card – either a credit card or a debit card drawn directly out of a bank account. Cheques are not at all common in Sweden and it is unlikely that many shops will accept one as payment.

If you want to return goods which you have bought at a shop, you have a few options. If you know you may want to return them when you buy them, make sure you tell the shop assistant. He or she will then write the words *öppet köp* on your receipt, and will tell you how many days you have to decide. This means literally 'open purchase' which will enable you to get a refund without any questions. If you do not ask for *öppet köp* then it is up to the goodwill of the shop owner; you do not have any rights of return unless the goods are damaged.

111

This is different from many shops worldwide, which offer no hassle refunds as a matter of course. Shops in Sweden which advertise a no hassle refund policy usually only honour this policy if you have asked for *öppet köp* in the first place.

However, if you are returning goods which are faulty or damaged, then you are protected under Swedish law, and must be offered either a refund or another item. Many electrical or mechanical goods are also sold with manufacturers' guarantees, so that if something subsequently breaks you can receive a replacement.

In general, shop assistants in Sweden are very helpful and many will either speak English or try to help you through sign language. You are often encouraged to try clothing on, to listen to CDs and tapes, or to try out sports equipment within the shop, before you buy, but it goes against Swedish nature to pressure you into buying anything.

Household Furnishings

So, where should you go to buy the things you need? If you need things for your house or flat, the first stop might be IKEA, as it is for most Swedes. IKEA is a Swedish chain of household furnishings which was founded in Småland in 1942 by Ingvar Kamprad. It has long been the most affordable place in Sweden to buy furniture, kitchen goods, fabric (for curtains and upholstery), kitchen and bathroom fittings, lighting and decorations. A warning here – no matter which branch you visit, it will be crowded every weekend. However, the service does tend to be helpful and you can take a lot of the furniture home with you (because it is often flatpack, self assembly furniture). If you can't, then they will deliver for free within a certain radius of the shop.

Other national shops which sell household goods include Åhléns (a general department store selling food, clothing, gifts and household goods) and, in Gothenburg and Stockholm, NK (short for Nordiska Kompaniet) which is rather more expensive. For china, glass, crockery, and other tableware, Duka is one of the best national shops. It is also an excellent place to buy gifts for Swedes or friends back home.

Another option is to frequent the auction houses and second hand shops. Most towns have at least one second hand shop which sells goods to raise money for *u-hjälpen* (assistance for the developing world) or for a church or athletic club. The furniture, crockery, clothing and so on ranges widely in quality, age and price, from expensive antiques to rickety old stools which need painting. You can often find many things you need much cheaper in the second hand shops.

CLOTHING

In general, Swedes dress quite casually, so the clothes you will probably need to buy first will not be dressy or formal clothes, but rather clothing to protect you against the weather and to help you live the active life many Swedes live. A good coat or jacket is essential, and so are good boots. The ones many Swedes wear are called *kängor* and are short sturdy boots, lined with wool or fur (though not as often these days) and with good soles for tramping on ice and through snow. You can buy these quite cheaply at Åhléns or at a shoe shop called Din Sko (which translates as 'Your Shoe'). Jackets and coats are sold in most clothing shops. Heavy waxed jackets (like Barbour or Drizabone) are also popular because, although it is cold in the winter, it does rain more than snow in the southern coastal cities (such as Malmö and Gothenburg).

As for what you will need if you are settling long term in Sweden – it is worth remembering that Swedes dress up only for special occasions. In some cities (such as the university towns of Lund and Uppsala), you might get some use out of a ball gown and dinner jacket or tuxedo. In most, however, you are unlikely ever to see anyone wearing them. The same goes for work clothes. Some industries dress up more than others, but it is not unusual to see people at work wearing jeans and a jumper.

Sports clothing, both for sports and leisure, is very popular and in general, American clothing is widely available and worn. Swedish sizes are the same as European sizes, and the clothing sold tends to be of a high quality. By Swedish law every piece of clothing sold must have a tag which gives the composition of the clothing along with instructions on how to wash it. Cotton and wool tend to be preferred to other fabrics, although leather is also popular for outerwear.

Quality and Price

Amongst the good buys in Sweden (in terms of quality and price) are sports clothes and equipment, including sailing and skiing goods. Amongst the not so good buys are shoes in general, which can be very expensive and not offer much choice. However, clogs come from Sweden. They are quite trendy internationally now but not in Sweden, where they are still seen as everyday basic shoes.

Other items which are very high quality are many hardware and electrical goods, especially those made by Electrolux and cameras by Hasselblad. The Swedish car industry is perceived as very expensive internationally, but Volvos and Saabs are certainly the most popular cars in Sweden. However, electrical goods are often very expensive in Sweden.

If you want to bring electrical goods with you from home, remember that Sweden uses 220-volt electricity. Many smaller goods, such as answering machines and video recorders, are built to different specifications in different countries, so they will not work with the Swedish television or telephone systems. Check this out with the manufacturer before you lug it to Sweden with you. Refrigerators, stoves and ovens are usually left in the house or flat when Swedes move, so you won't need to ship those over. It is worth remembering, too, that Swedish houses are sized smaller than houses in some countries, such as North America, and some appliances won't fit!

WHAT TO TAKE HOME WITH YOU

Sweden is famous for its glass and wooden goods worldwide, and you will find many beautiful examples wherever you go. If you get a chance, do travel to the Glasriket area of Sweden, near Växjö in Småland, where you can visit many of the most famous glassmakers, such as Kosta Boda, or Orrefors and buy first or second quality goods. Wine glasses, vases, plates and bowls or sculptures are all available; not much of it is cheap but it is all beautiful and often cheaper here than elsewhere.

If you prefer wooden handicrafts, you might choose between a handpainted Dala horse, a butter knife, or a cheese/sandwich board. The horse,which comes in many sizes, has almost come to be a symbol of Sweden, although in fact it is only made in the region of Dalarna. The knives and boards are still widely used in Sweden.

Other typically Swedish goods are ceramics, silverware and amber jewellery, pewter (especially made up in classic Viking designs), Saami handicrafts and textiles. A *toarpkronan,* which is an iron chandelier decorated with flags and ribbons, is often found in Swedish homes and makes a very unusual and lovely gift. The national handicrafts organisation, *Svenska hemslöjdsföreningarnas riksförbund,* endorses certain examples of Swedish crafts; these are marked with a round sticker with the words *Svensk slöjd* on it.

The *Jokkmokk* market, in far northern Sweden, is held in February every year and if you can manage to get up to Jokkmokk you will have the opportunity to buy many authentic Saami handicrafts and foods. If you buy Saami handicrafts elsewhere, look out for the *Duodji,* label which is a mark of its authenticity. A final place to visit to buy Swedish souvenirs is the Rörstrand china factory in Lidköping, where you can find wonderful Swedish china at lower than retail prices.

Chapter Seven

A YEAR IN SWEDEN

FESTIVALS AND HOLIDAYS

Traditionally, the year in Sweden revolved around the Church year. Although not many Swedes are devout churchgoers now, most of the important Church festivals are still observed and many are public holidays.

The Church year begins with Advent, which starts on the fourth Sunday before Christmas. On the first Sunday in Advent, many Swedes go to church and get together for a meal afterwards or in the evening. It is almost the beginning of the Christmas season, and people start to think about buying presents, planning parties and decorating their homes. Decorations will already have gone up in the shopping centres (probably by early November in fact). December is dominated by Christmas and also by Lucia Day. On children's television there is a *julkalender*, which has a special show for each day in December leading up to Christmas, and many children open Advent calendars, coloured paper pictures which have small windows to open for each day from the 1st to the 24th. Behind each window is another picture, or a small present or chocolate.

Lucia Day

On December 13, Sweden celebrates Lucia Day. The day is traditionally in honour of St. Lucia from Sicily, but the day's celebrations today have little to do with her or any religious observance. There are three levels of celebration in most places. In many families the youngest daughter (or child) dresses up as Lucia, with a long white robe and a wreath of candles on her head, and wakes her family up with the song *"Sankta Lucia"* and coffee and saffron buns *(lussekatter*, specially made for Lucia Day), very early in the morning. Of course, in most families, at least one parent is already up to make the coffee and get the saffron buns out for the child, and so it is often the father of the family who lies awake in bed waiting to be 'awoken' by the little Lucia, but it is a much loved tradition.

Even if you do not celebrate Lucia Day at home, you may well see it at its second level, in many schools and workplaces. In many offices the employees will start the day with coffee, saffron buns and gingersnaps *(pepparkakor)* rather than going straight to work, and schools will often pick a Lucia and attendants and have their own small celebration. The Lucias can have as many female attendants (called *Luciatärnor)* and male attendants (called *stjärngossar*, or star boys) as they like, so all pupils can take part.

Finally, Lucia is celebrated on a local and national level as every local newspaper will have a competition to pick a Lucia for the town that year. These Lucias will usually lead a parade through town, and then spend much time during the Christmas season bringing saffron buns and gingersnaps to homes for the elderly and hospitals. Most of these Lucias are in their early twenties and invariably have long blonde hair! There is also an official Lucia for Sweden and many unofficial television Lucias, often filmed waking up famous people. It is a fun festival, mostly for children, but welcomed by everyone as a way of bringing light to a very dark time of the year.

Christmas

After Lucia the country really gears itself up for Christmas, and most homes put up decorations including an Advent star (a large six pointed star with a light in the middle) and an electric candelabra in the window to light up the night. Many homes change their curtains and put out a myriad of other decorations as well, and put up a Christmas tree in the week before Christmas. You can buy an artificial tree but most families buy a real tree cut down specially for Christmas. In December they are sold on many street corners so they are not difficult to find. Other popular Christmas plants are red poinsettias, tulips and begonias, as well as white, blue and pink hyacinths. It is common to send Christmas cards to friends and relatives in time for Christmas, especially if you will not see them, and to exchange gifts with relatives. Preparations for Christmas also include lots of cooking and baking, making of gingerbread houses and tree decorations, wrapping of presents, and, finally, travelling to relatives' homes to celebrate with them.

The actual festival begins at lunchtime on the 24th. Most work-places and shops will close on the evening of the 23rd, and children finish school the week before for two weeks holiday. Many Swedes eat a traditional light meal of broth and bread for lunch and then settle down in front of the television to watch an omnibus edition of Disney cartoons for a few hours. This programme has been on the television for years and repeats every Christmas Eve, but is still incredibly popular as a Christmas tradition.

In the evening many families dress up and the real celebrations begin, with a big *julbord* (Christmas buffet table) of traditional Christmas foods, including several types of herring salads, liver paste, smoked sausages, a large ham and *lutfisk*, a dried fish marinated in lye (a rather acquired taste for a non-Swede) and is served with a white sauce or butter. Afterwards, rice pudding with either cinnamon or jam is served, and whoever finds the hidden almond has to say a rice pudding rhyme in some households, or will be the next to marry in others. (The traditions alter in different regions.)

After dinner the *jultomten* (literally, Christmas gnome, but actually a Father Christmas/Santa Claus figure) comes in with his red hat and white beard (but a red robe rather than suit) to distribute presents from a sack on his back. Unlike Santa Claus, however, the *jultomten* comes in through the door (the fireplace, if there is one, probably has a fire in it!) and asks directly, "Are there any good children here?" Christmas presents in Sweden are called *julklapp*, or 'Christmas tap,' from the Middle Ages when people would sneak up to houses, tap on the door and quickly put a present inside and run away again. Family members will also give presents to each other, and these are often put underneath the tree until Christmas Eve.

On Christmas Day many go to an early morning church service, called *jullottan*, which often starts at 7:00 a.m. and ends before dawn. It is a beautiful candlelit service with much singing, and is popular with churchgoers and non-churchgoers alike. After the service it is time to eat some more and enjoy the new presents, but Christmas celebrations are over for another year. However, the day after Christmas is a public holiday, and many Swedes have time off to spend with their families, and go skiing (if there is snow so early) and celebrate.

New Year

As in many countries, New Year's Eve is greatly celebrated with parties, champagne and fireworks throughout Sweden. Christmas food is still served, but the parties are now more for friends than for families. Every year on television there is a repeat of "The Duchess and the Butler," a little known English television sketch which many Swedes know off by heart and, just before midnight, a reading of Alfred Tennyson's "New Year's Clock" (in Swedish of course!) which ends just as the clock starts to strike twelve. In the cities lots of people go out to watch the fireworks, in spite of freezing temperatures, and go on eating, drinking and dancing into the small hours, knowing that they can sleep in on New Year's Day.

Three Kings Day and the End of Christmas

But the Christmas/New Year holidays are not over yet. There is another holiday on January 6, Epiphany, when the three wise men reached Bethlehem (called *Trettondagen* – Thirteenth Day, or *Heliga tre konungars dag*, – Three Kings Day). In most countries it is also the day to take down the Christmas decorations, but in Sweden they are left up for another week, to come down on January 13, or *tjugondag Knut* (20th Day Knut). This may be for several reasons; Swedes joke it is because they like Christmas more than other nations, and that they have such dark nights they need the Christmas lights, but it is more likely because the Vikings held a mid winter feast on this day, and the early Church in Sweden tried to stop the pagan festivities by making January 13 part of Christmas. In any case, this is the day to take down all of the decorations and clean up after the festivities. A *julgransplundring* party, when the tree is stripped of its decorations and the last of the Christmas food is eaten up, is common amongst Swedes, especially for children, and is a good way to make a tiring task fun.

Sportlov – The Sports Holiday

The next big holiday for children (and for all adults with children) is the school break in February, which is a wintersports holiday. Many families do go skiing in this week, although you have to book for the popular ski resorts in Sweden and in the Alps early. It is becoming more common to go to a warm climate for this week, as well. The weeks are staggered for different regions throughout Sweden, so that not every schoolchild is free during the same week, although Swedish ski resorts are still crowded during most of February.

Fastlag – Shrove Tuesday

The six weeks before Easter (in late March or April) were traditionally weeks to avoid meat and fats, and so the last day before Lent begins, which is always on a Wednesday, is called Fat Tuesday in many countries. In Sweden it is a day to eat *semlor*, buns which are filled with marzipan and whipped cream (also called *fettisbullar* and *fastlagsbullar*) which were traditionally served in a bowl of warm milk with cinnamon. Now many eat them as they are, and they are available right up until Easter, thus defeating the original object of eating up the fat in the house! Not many Swedes hold to the Lenten fast any longer and they prefer to enjoy *semlor* for as long as possible.

Waffle Day

Not a proper holiday, but many Swedes do still eat waffles on March 25. The reason is not religious or traditional, but only because this is the Day of the Virgin Mary in the Church, which in Swedish is called *Vår Fru Dag* (literally, Our Lady Day) and the faster one says *Vår Fru*, the more it sounds like *Våffel*, or waffle – a good excuse to eat waffles in schools and many homes!

Easter

Easter, the holiest festival in the Church year, means a four day break for most Swedes and two weeks for schoolchildren, during the time of year when the country is just coming out of winter. Again, many Swedes decorate their homes, changing to yellow or pink curtains and tablecloths, and putting birch twigs with brightly coloured feathers tied to them (called *påskris*) around their homes. Daffodils (called

Easter lilies in Sweden) and tulips in pastel colours are also popular, and it is often time for a thorough spring cleaning before the family comes to visit for Easter.

A family celebrating a more traditional Easter would have an Easter dinner of eggs and lamb on Saturday evening (the day before Easter) after having eaten fish on Good Friday. Any small girls in the house will dress up as brightly coloured witches, with headshawls and long skirts, and will go around to the neighbours asking for Easter treats (usually chocolates, sweets or small change). Witches are not associated with Easter in many other countries, but in Sweden the association comes from an ancient belief that during Easter the witches went to visit the devil at Blåkulla, and it was important to keep them from coming near one's own house whilst on their journeys. In some parts of Sweden people light bonfires on Easter Saturday to keep the witches away. Swedes also enjoy eating Easter chocolates and sweets, and painting eggshells in bright colours for decorations. However, for most Swedes these festivities are only a part of Easter. The four-day break from work is well timed to do a lot of early spring gardening, to begin to get the boat ready for the summer season, or to open up the summer house for the first time in the year. Still other Swedes take the opportunity to get in some of the last skiing of the year or to go abroad for a holiday.

Walpurgis Night – Valborgmässoafton

Soon after Easter comes April 30, when people get together in crowds to sing and have large bonfires. This is not a public holiday, but is the evening before the first day of May, which is one, so that Swedes know they can stay out late and sleep in the next day. The bonfires are again to frighten off witches and evil spirits going to visit the devil and are more common in Stockholm and the east than on the west coast where bonfires are more common at Easter. The holiday traditions are mixed together with traditional student celebrations of the beginning of spring on May 1, common in Uppsala and Lund.

In Gothenburg also there is a parade put on by students at Chalmers University with lots of floats and funny costumes; a very popular way to spend the early evening for both young and old. Many students and former students wear the white caps they earned by completing gymnasium on April 30.

May Days

Traditionally the first day of May was the beginning of spring and was therefore a day off, but since the late 19th century the gatherings in parks and city centres have been to mark International Labour Day, when many of the unions and workers march in the streets to commemorate workers' rights. They are joined by bands, orchestras and politicians giving speeches. Further public holidays in May are Ascension Day, the day in the Church calendar when Christ ascended into heaven (*Kristi himmelsfärds dag*), which is five and a half weeks after Easter, and always on a Thursday.

Whitsunday and Whitmonday (*Pingstdagen* and *Annandag Pingst*), are celebrated a week and a half after Ascension Day. Because Ascension Day is on a Thursday many Swedes take the Friday off as well for a long weekend of gardening, sailing, or just relaxing at their summer houses. The three day weekend of Whitsunday, on the other hand, is a traditional time for weddings. The last Sunday in May is Mother's Day, when mothers and grandmothers receive cards, flowers and sometimes presents or chocolates from their families.

Flag Day

Sweden for a long time had no national day until, during the First World War, some Swedes began privately to celebrate the Swedish flag day on June 6, which was the anniversary of the day that Gustav Vasa was chosen as the first Swedish king in 1523, and also of the day that one of the Swedish constitutions was signed in 1809. From 1916, more and more Swedes began to observe the day with parades and

123

public gatherings, but it is a normal workday, and the average Swede celebrates it only by raising the Swedish flag on the flagpole in his or her garden. The flag day was officially named the national day in 1983.

The End of the School Year

In many nations this is merely a relief for pupils and students, but in Sweden it is a day for parties and celebrations in the middle of June. Every level of school will have an assembly where the pupils dress up and sing summer songs, such as "The Time of Flowers is Coming" (*Den Blomstertid nu Kommer*, Hymn 474 in the Swedish hymnal), hear talks from their teachers, and celebrate the beginning of summer and the end of another school year.

They will not have to return until the second or third week in August. For students who are finishing secondary school, or *gymnasium*, at the age of 18 or 19, it is an even bigger celebration. They wear

Students celebrate the end of their gymnasium *years with parties. The car takes them through town to show everyone they've finished. The caps, or* studentmössor, *show that they have graduated.*

their white student caps with their best clothing all day, and take part in a special school assembly, often with prize giving, student musicians, drama performances and art shows, and good luck talks from teachers and head teachers. As the assembly finishes, parents gather outside the school gates bearing flowers, champagne, and large signs with baby photographs and names of their grownup children. The students often drive in groups around the town or city in open top cars, shouting and laughing all the time, or have special family parties, or head off to balls and parties in the evening, or enjoy all three types of celebrations. They are often very wild but it is their special day and nobody else minds.

Midsummer's Day

This is, along with Christmas, one of the biggest holidays on the Swedish calendar, and one of the only ones which is particularly Swedish. It is celebrated on the Friday and Saturday of the week closest to June 24, which is the real Midsummer's Day, and incorporates pagan summer solstice celebrations.

It is a holiday to be out in the country, and to celebrate the long days of summer. Even in the south of Sweden there are more than 18 hours of daylight at this time of the year, and in the north the sun does not really set at all. For children the holiday begins in the afternoon, when the midsummer pole decorated with flowers and ribbons is raised. There are a few different theories about the midsummer pole, which is called a *majstång* or *midsommarstång* in Swedish. One is that it has always been raised at midsummer and that the *maj* in the name stems from an old Nordic word meaning decorated. Another is that the tradition stems from the German maypole, which was raised on the first of May to celebrate the good weather. In most of Sweden this is too early to celebrate good weather, so the tradition was moved to midsummer. Suffice it to say that it is now a definite symbol of midsummer, and many Swedes raise their own in their gardens for their own family parties.

Photo: Robert Grahm

A traditional midsummer pole. The parents and children standing around are waiting for the singing and games around the midsummer pole to begin, with music from the folk band.

When the midsummer pole is up, the children sing songs and dance traditional dances and games, pretending to be small frogs and other animals. As the afternoon turns into evening it becomes time for the adults to celebrate. The menu for all is decided by tradition; new potatoes boiled with dill, several kinds of herring in sauces, beer and *snaps* to drink and strawberries with cream for afterwards. After the meal the parties and dancing continue, often past sunrise the next day (but remember that sunrise can be as early as three o'clock in the morning). Traditionally unmarried girls would pick seven or nine different wild flowers and sleep with them under their pillows, in order to dream of the men they would marry. Midsummer is also a popular time for engagements and weddings.

SUMMER IN SWEDEN

After midsummer, most Swedes have only a week left of work before Sweden shuts down for the summer holidays. Many factories and workplaces close for four weeks in July, and Swedes leave the cities and towns for small country houses on the sea and lakes. This is the time when they take the opportunity to enjoy the countryside and nature, during the warmest and lightest month of the year. Others travel abroad, to Mediterranean resorts and further afield. Intensive language courses in other countries are popular for adults, but most prefer to relax in the countryside with their families and friends. Summer camps and schools for children, as in the United States, are not common and most families do holiday together.

Crayfish Parties – The End of Summer

In August the holidays are drawing to a close, the days are already getting shorter and cooler and children go back to school. But it is also time for crayfish *(kräftor)* parties and, soon after that, *surströmming* parties in the north of Sweden.

Crayfish parties began over a hundred years ago, when the crayfish season was limited in Sweden and people wanted to celebrate being able to eat crayfish again. Traditionally they should be held on the night of the first full moon after the beginning of the season, and they are jolly and informal parties, with piles of boiled crayfish, sauces to go with them, beer and *snaps*. The eating, drinking, reciting of crayfish rhymes and singing goes on until late at night. Crayfish are very messy to eat and you can buy paper bibs, napkins and even hats with pictures of crayfish on them, specially for these parties. The Swedish crayfish has nearly been fished out of existence, so most of the crayfish eaten at the parties are imported from Turkey, Spain or the US. You can buy frozen crayfish throughout the year but a crayfish party is a wonderful excuse to get together and eat and drink lots!

The *surströmming*, or fermented herring, parties are really only in the north of Sweden, but they are fascinating to the rest of Sweden. The fish is a very acquired taste, and takes a year to mature. In mid-August they are ready, and Swedes in the north get together to eat them with 'thin bread,' small northern potatoes and lots of beer and *snaps*. Anyone who does not like *surstömming* will tell you that they need to drink a lot to cope with the taste and smell.

A tradition in the south of Sweden, is that of *ålagille*, or eel feasts. When the August moon begins to wane and the nights get darker, the eels cannot see the nets and are easily caught. These are eaten in many forms; fried, boiled, smoked and stuffed with different fillings. They are very rich with fat, and so the feasters wash them down with a few *snaps*. (Of course!)

128

All Saints Day

After the summer, Swedes settle back into work and school and get ready for the long winter. There are no more special holidays or celebrations until November 1, All Saints Day, which is a solemn day for remembering the dead. It is one of the public holidays which never moves, so if the 1st is on a Saturday or Sunday there is no break from work. School children do have a week's holiday around this time – they have already been studying for more than two months by now.

St. Martin's Day

November 10 is St. Martin's Day, a day celebrated not for the saint himself but for the geese which are eaten traditionally on this day. This particular tradition began in France, St. Martin's homeland, centuries ago, and spread first to Germany and then to Sweden around the 1500s.

It is when the geese are plumpest, and also when the year's wine is ready to be drunk (in France at least). In the southern province of Skåne many Swedes go to restaurants to eat black soup (made traditionally with goose or pig blood, but now often with stock), roast goose and apple cake or *spettekaka*, a tall cake of egg yolks and sugar, baked on a spit. This is a meal Skåne-dwellers eat with pride, but in fact it originated in a restaurant in Stockholm in the 1850s, with influences from the cooking of Renaissance France. Following St. Martin's Day there are only a few weeks until the first Sunday in Advent, and the country begins decorating and baking for Christmas again.

OTHER CELEBRATIONS

Like most other nationalities, Swedes celebrate birthdays, births and marriages and will gather together for funerals. It is common for children to have a birthday party *(kalas)* every year, and they are usually in their own homes, not in restaurants or theme parks. The mother of the birthday child bakes a cake and the children bring presents for the birthday child and play games. If your child is invited to such a party you are not expected to be there as well – Swedes are comfortable with allowing their children to go to parties without them. Many Swedes do have 'name days' as well, but they are not celebrated in the way they are in some countries.

As children become adults they are less likely to have parties for their birthdays except for 'even' birthdays, when they turn 30, 40, 50 or 60. This custom was originally only for the 50th birthday, and that is still the most important celebration, but many get together with friends and family for eating, drinking, singing and dancing on their 30th and 40th birthdays as well. The American custom of a big party on the 16th birthday and the British and Australian custom of a big party on the 21st birthday are not common in Sweden.

Other celebrations are often more family oriented. Most babies born in Sweden today are still christened, and the parents will invite their families to a meal after the church service, but Swedes do not have large christening parties. Seventy-five percent of Swedes choose to be confirmed in the Church of Sweden in their early teens, and that is another occasion for a family celebration with a cake and gifts.

Weddings

Weddings, on the other hand, combine a mixture of family and friends for the church service (still the most popular option) and the dinner and dancing afterwards. The celebrations are similar to those in many other European countries, with sparkling wine, flowers and a traditional bridal waltz to start the dancing. One big difference is that in Sweden the couple will often have lived together for many years, and their children may also be at the wedding, perhaps as flower-girls or pageboys. In the run up to the wedding the bride's friends will often have planned a hen night *(möhippa)* for her and the groom's friends a stag night *(svensexa)* for him, at which both will be given lots to drink and have any number of practical jokes played on them. The day of these parties is a surprise for the bride and groom and, unlike some

A Swedish bride and groom sit under their bridal wreath at the top of the table.

countries, the bride and groom never plan their own parties. (Nor can they escape the ones their friends plan for them!)

On the Sunday before the wedding the couple may have a *lysning*, which comes from the now defunct tradition of listening to the wedding banns in church and having a meal with presents afterwards. If you are invited to a *lysning* you take the couple's wedding present to that party and not to the wedding itself, and it is usually a daytime party with a meal and a few drinks.

On the day of the actual wedding the bride's family traditionally will welcome the guests to the church, and during the service the bride and groom will walk up the aisle to the altar together, instead of the bride and her father meeting the groom at the altar. They will have exchanged two rings at their engagement, and the bride will usually receive a second gold band during the ceremony. After the service the couple stands outside the church and all of the guests walk past them and congratulate them. The reception is usually at another hall or restaurant, where the couple arrive last and are toasted with sparkling wine by their guests. They sit under a bridal arch of flowers during the meal, which is interrupted often by speeches and songs. After the meal the bridal couple may open their presents at the reception, and they will almost certainly waltz together before everyone else joins in. They do not usually disappear before the guests, as in a British wedding, but stay and enjoy the party until late.

Many couples go away on a honeymoon, but this is called a 'wedding trip' in Sweden, whereas the Swedish for honeymoon, *smekmånad*, refers to the first month of marriage no matter where you are. When they return they are likely to send printed thank you cards to their guests, with a wedding photo of themselves on it.

Socialising with Swedes – Dinner Parties

Swedes are not as open about inviting people home as many other nationalities, so don't worry if it takes a while before you get any invitations. It probably doesn't mean you are unpopular and eventually, when you know your colleagues or friends a bit better, you are likely to be invited over.

The invitations are usually verbal except for formal or special occasions. Sometimes a written invitation will have the letters O.S.A. and a telephone number at the bottom, which means you should ring to tell the hosts whether you will be able to attend or not. On the day of the party it is important to be punctual. There are jokes about Swedes waiting on the doorstep for five minutes in order to be able to ring the doorbell at 7:00 p.m. prompt – you may find that this actually happens in Sweden. In any case if you are invited for 7:00 p.m. for a meal, the host or hostess will have planned for the food to be ready then or soon afterwards, so it would be rude to keep them waiting. The custom of 20 minutes late being polite is not practised in Sweden.

Most guests bring a small present for the host and hostess, such as chocolates, wine or flowers. If you bring flowers it is considered polite to take off the paper or plastic wrapping before handing them over. Unless the party is in a public place you will remove the shoes you wore outside at the door, and either pad about in socks or else change into party shoes which you have carried in your bag. This is purely practical; it keeps floors clean longer throughout the year, but is very important in the snowy and muddy winter and spring seasons. When you arrive you will probably be offered a welcome drink, often a kind of alcoholic punch, or else perhaps a cup of *glögg* at Christmas time. After that the drink often switches to beer or wine to have with the food.

Swedes, after they have given flowers to their hostess, taken their shoes off and accepted their welcome drink, will usually greet the other guests in turn. If they are already acquainted or friends, this is just a simple *Hej* and perhaps a handshake. If not, then they will introduce themselves at the time. The onus for introductions is on the arriving guests, not the host or hostess, so it is important not to miss your time to introduce yourself. At any semiformal or seated dinner party the guests are likely to be given places, or at least asked to sit alternating male and female, and not near their partners. At any meal, whether formal or family, Swedes will thank the cook for the meal, saying usually *Tack för maten* (literally, 'Thanks for the food'). At dinner parties with more than eight guests it is traditionally the job of the male seated to the left of the hostess to thank her for the meal on behalf of all the guests with a small speech.

Toasting

During any festive meal there are likely to be glasses of *snaps* and much toasting or *skåling* in Swinglish. The anatomy of a *skål* is very specific; you should lift your glass and nod at everyone at the table in turn, going from right to left, before taking a drink (sometimes a sip and sometimes the whole glass, depending on the drink, the occasion and the company). After the drink you should nod at the others again before putting the glass down. In practice this is often rather rushed through, otherwise it can take a long time.

At a formal party nobody should propose a toast before the host does, and women should not drink before the man seated to their left (their dinner companion for the evening) has proposed a toast to her. This is important, particularly if you plan to attend any very formal dinners. At most dinners the host does propose a welcome toast (with the welcome drink, of course) first, but women and men both drink – and *skål* – when they choose.

At a festive meal you are likely to eat a *smörgåsbord*. Of course you could eat from the buffet in any order you choose, but the standard order is to start with the fish, move on to the meat and then the hot dishes and then finish with the cheese. The rules to remember are, fish before meat and cold before hot. At any meal you should finish the food on your plate, but no one should take the last bit of food in the serving dish.

After the meal, and the thank you for it, there is often a break before dessert is served with coffee. This is usually enough to allow stomachs to recover from the food. If at someone's home, everyone will withdraw to the living room and probably eat the dessert there. It is not unusual for Swedes to sing at any party, either drinking songs (*snapsvisor*) or special songs for the time of year. You might hear one popular drinking song, called *"Helan Går,"* (The whole thing goes) if you are with Swedes who enjoy drinking their *snaps* (in other words, most Swedes). The song is very short, and goes:

> *Helan går, sjung hopp falle rallan rallan lej, helan går, sjung hopp falle rallan lej. Och den some inte helan tar, han heller into halvan får. Helan går, sjung hopp falle rallan lej.*

In translation this means, the whole thing goes, and if you don't drink the whole thing, you won't get half again! When you hear this song it's time to drink the whole *snaps* glass down. Women and foreigners can avoid this task rather more easily than Swedish men, which is just as well as some of the *snaps* can taste very bitter and all are very strong.

When it is time to leave you should put on your coat and shoes before you thank your host, though you will have said goodbye to the other guests beforehand. The next time you communicate with your hosts, whether in person, by phone or by letter, you should tell them, "Thank you for last time" *(tack för senast)*. This is true even if you don't see them again for a month. To be very polite you should write a special thank you or ring specially to thank your hosts within a week, though this is much less important than saying *tack för senast*.

Coffee and Cake Parties

These are very popular parties in Sweden, for birthdays, name-days, in fact any day you feel like inviting people over. They are perhaps an equivalent to 'taking tea' in Britain. However, you are unlikely to have any sandwiches, just coffee and cakes. Traditionally there will be seven cakes on offer. It's no good pleading a small appetite, to be polite you must take one of each, and at the beginning of the party. Balancing seven small cakes (often the same size as biscuits or cookies) on one plate is easy compared to eating them all if you've eaten a meal before. Enjoy them – they are almost certainly home-baked and delicious.

Remember, whenever you drink coffee with Swedes that many do not take milk with their coffee, and will pour coffee into your cup to the rim if you don't remind them to leave some space in the cup for your milk or cream.

Chapter Eight

BEYOND BERGMAN AND ABBA

THE ARTS IN SWEDEN

Beyond the pop group Abba, so popular in the 1970s, and the films of Ingmar Bergman, giving a rather depressing view of Sweden, the arts and music of Sweden are little known in the rest of the world. A few people may also know the playwright August Strindberg, the actress Greta Garbo, and perhaps the artist Carl Larsson. We've already seen in earlier chapters that Swedes are hard workers and love the outdoors and sports; perhaps there is not as much interest in the fine and performing arts and in literature as in other countries, such as France or Italy.

Fortunately, this is not at all the case. It's simply that Sweden is a much smaller country in terms of population, and also that Swedish is a 'small' language with few speakers. Many talented filmmakers, writers and musical groups who are very popular at home find it difficult to break into the international arena. You will most likely learn about these artists and enjoy their work, especially when you are more comfortable speaking Swedish.

Support for the Arts

The arts in Sweden are subsidised and supported by both the state and large corporations. The state funds grants to libraries, theatres, the opera and publishers, among others. Newspapers and magazines are also subsidised, as are specific art exhibitions and performances. To help everyone in such a 'spread-out' country enjoy the arts, the National Travelling Theatre *(Riksteatern)* performs all over the country in different towns and cities. For big international performances you may have to travel to Stockholm, Göteborg or Malmö, but many of these will be sponsored for travel to smaller towns.

As well as this, every county has its own museum *(länsmuseum)* with arts and history from that region. There are many excellent museums in the larger cities, and the entrance fees, where they exist at all, are low because of state support. The national museums are in Stockholm, with the country's artistic, design and historical treasures, but many smaller, interesting museums are dotted about the country in smaller cities.

The biggest theatres and dance troupes are, again, in the big cities. However, many of the groups travel throughout the country, and amateur dramatics and dance are very popular. English-speaking theatre makes an appearance from time to time, either with visiting groups or local English-speakers. Look out for special performances, such as *Hamlet* performed in a medieval castle, or the street theatre during Stockholm's water festival. If you are interested in participating, look in your local newspaper where many amateur groups advertise, especially those that are arranged by study circle groups. All different kinds of dance are popular in Sweden, though folk and ballroom dancing hold a special place in the Swedish heart.

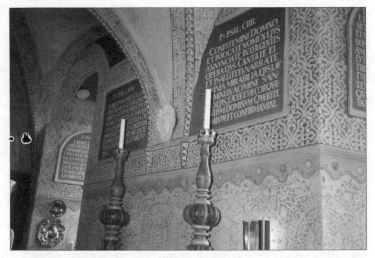

The decorations inside Kalmar Castle are some of the best examples of early Swedish painting.

MUSIC

Part of the reason dance is popular is because Swedes are a very musical people. You can hear that in their accents when they speak! But joking apart, most Swedes enjoy singing, whether in an organised group, as a performer, or simply with friends at a celebratory party. One of the most famous Swedish singers was Jenny Lind, the opera singer called the 'Swedish Nightingale' who enchanted audiences internationally in the 19th century. She is honoured in Sweden with her picture on the 50 crown note.

Today, singing in a choir, religious or secular, is one of the most popular hobbies in Sweden. At parties guests will often sing special songs for the occasion, beginning with children's songs at birthday parties, midsummer and Christmas, and reaching a height of merriment with the *snapsvisor* (drinking songs) sung to help glasses of strong alcohol down at adult parties. When attending a special occasion, such as a 50th birthday party or a wedding, it's common for

Swedes to make up a special song in honour of the celebrations. They'll sing it a cappella, or with a guitar or piano, and it becomes an integral part of celebrating.

Folk Music

Folk music, like folk dancing, is important to Swedes. Every county and area has its own music and songs. Much of the music is based on the fiddle, and is meant for dancing. Several composers in the late 19th century were inspired by traditional Swedish folk music, among them Wilhelm Peterson-Berger and Hugo Alfvén. Their music plays on the national soul even today, truly a part of the Swedish psyche.

Music, singing and dancing remain popular to this day. Swedish dance-band music is heard everywhere and spans the generations. It is something of an acquired taste, and sounds not unlike the dance music popular in many countries in the 1950s. However, all types of music have their following in Sweden. Classical music is represented by several world-class symphonic orchestras, while there are regular jazz festivals throughout the country. Indeed, such groups as the Esbjorn Svensson Trio tour to great acclaim internationally.

Popular Music

In the past thirty years the Swedish rock and pop groups have been immensely popular both at home and overseas. Abba (made up of Anni-Frid, Benny, Björn and Agneta – hence the name) won the Eurovision Song Contest in 1974 with "Waterloo" and went on to be one of the most popular groups ever. Like many Swedish groups, they had both Swedish and English versions of their songs. The groups of today tend to sing only in English, as they aim for a bigger market from the beginning. The success of groups such as Ace of Base, Roxette and The Cardigans has earned a great deal of money for the Swedish economy. Indeed, Ace of Base broke all of the records with their album, Happy Nation, which sold over 20 million copies worldwide – the biggest sales ever for a first album. The group is

Photo: Robert Grahm

Although rock, pop and dance music are popular in Sweden, the old folk music, played at midsummer and other summer holidays, has never lost its appeal for Swedes.

criticised for producing 'middle-of-the-road' pop music in Sweden but perhaps this is another case of cutting down tall poppies – nobody should be too successful!

DESIGN AND ARCHITECTURE

Throughout its history, functionalism has been important for Swedes, but everyday objects should also look good. The sleek lines of a Saab car, the clean medicine-bottle shape of an Absolut Vodka bottle, are part of the functionality of these useful things. Swedes appreciate simplicity, and much of Swedish (and Scandinavian) design is very sophisticated in its minimalism. However, this minimalism isn't necessarily worked towards – it's simply what Swedes agree looks good.

Modern architecture has benefited from functional concepts, but some think it went too far in the 1960s and 1970s, and many new houses built today follow the traditional lines of the red farmhouses built in Sweden throughout the centuries. Amongst the innovators (or culprits, depending on how you look at it) in modern architecture have been Gunnar Asplund and Ivar Tengbom, who both worked in the early 20th century. Their designs for community buildings, such as libraries and concert halls, were based on the ideals of functionalism and simplicity.

CRAFTS

The love of good design which works and doesn't look cluttered extends to many other arts and crafts popular in Sweden. Several of these, notably ceramics, glass and textiles, have grown into large industries with well established overseas markets. Sturdy pottery looks wonderful and is popular, but the fine porcelain made by companies such as Rörstrand and Gustavsberg matches any made by other fine china-makers. Textile companies tend to concentrate on luxury fabrics and the traditional woven cloths of Sweden are beautifully designed and created.

Meanwhile, the great glass-blowing companies of Småland, such as Kosta Boda and Orrefors, create both luxury and everyday glass items for the world market. Glass-blowing came to Sweden with a Venetian and has been an important industry ever since. Many of the styles remain the same as they were a hundred years ago, with cut crystal and simple straight lines equally popular. However, the glass companies employ many younger designers who create beautiful, colourful and modern designs that are both functional and decorative. You don't have to go to Småland to see glass-blowing or buy original works, there are many smaller glass-blowers throughout the country and the beautiful glass is on sale throughout Sweden.

Many of the old-fashioned crafts which are less common in other countries are still popular in Sweden. Back in the 1950s, an English visitor observed, "In most countries, the magic of the all powerful machine rapidly drove ancient handicraft traditions beyond recall. Sweden, however, was luckier. Here, the indigenous peasant craft was rescued in the very nick of time, just as it was on the brink of disappearing forever. Thus the people never quite lost their century old designs, nor the feel of raw material in their hands." *(The Charm of Sweden*, 1956).

Swedish children learn handicrafts in school and knitting, embroidery, and woodcarving remain hobbies for many into adult life. Less common, but with a large following, are the crafts of weaving, lace-making, rug-making, candle-making and smithery.

Those who don't enjoy such crafts appreciate being able to buy handmade items. You can, of course, always buy cheap imitations made abroad. In spite of the expense, however, many Swedes prefer to buy the real handmade and carefully designed goods.

ART

In addition to an appreciation for handicrafts and good design, Swedes appreciate fine arts, with painting and sculpture having a special popularity amongst Swedish artists. While visiting art galleries and collecting works of art at auction is fashionable in the larger cities, even in rural areas a Swede is more likely to hang an original painting on the wall than a reproduction, and art appreciation evening classes are popular.

Swedish artistic trends were heavily influenced by European trends throughout the Middle Ages and Renaissance, with ornate wall painting, murals and decorations giving way to portraiture in the late 15th and early 16th centuries. The baroque and rococo styles popular in Europe in the 16th and 17th centuries influenced the Gustavian period of the 18th century. The Gustavian style, also called Swedish Neo-Classicism, is growing in popularity again today, with ornate furniture and decorations in simple surroundings and colours, reminiscent of Greek and Roman antiquity.

By the 19th century, artists were inspired by a more defined Nordic style, with classical and romantic painters choosing Norse mythology and Swedish history as subjects. By the late 19th and early

20th century, the national trend towards romanticism fostered a return to simplicity in the arts. Sculptors such as Carl Milles and Stig Blomberg and painters such as Carl Larsson, Bruno Liljefors and Anders Zorn all flourished at this time.

Modern Art

Anders Zorn is considered one of the most gifted Swedish painters but Carl Larsson also deserves a special mention. His watercolours and bright illustrations depict a romantic view of everyday life in the Swedish countryside. Larsson's work is still popular today, perhaps more so than 20 years ago, as many Swedes idealise the simplicity of the agrarian lifestyle of days gone by.

In the 20th century, artistic trends ranging from Cubism and Surrealism to Neo-Realism and Primitivism have all been represented in Sweden as they have throughout Europe. As in other countries, many younger artists prefer to concentrate on graphic and industrial design rather than classical painting and sculpture. However, state support means that new art, some traditional and some very experimental, is bought and displayed in public buildings (such as galleries and libraries). It's not all equally appreciated by the public, but ensures that the fine arts, from folk art and impressionism to modern and graphical art, remain very much a part of Swedish life.

FILM

Amongst the most famous Swedes abroad must always be counted the actresses Ingrid Bergman and Greta Garbo, both famous in Hollywood films earlier this century. However, there are many other Swedes, both behind and in front of the camera, who have contributed to the international film industry.

Among the first were Mauritz Stiller and Victor Sjöström, both directors who went to Hollywood in the 1930s. They were followed by one of the greatest directors of all, Ingmar Bergman. His films tackle serious questions of existentialism, religion and conscience.

Many of his films were produced in the 1950s and 1960s (he was born in 1918), but are still shown today, particularly his classics such as *The Seventh Seal* and *Through a Glass Darkly*. His last film, *Fanny and Alexander*, came out in 1982 – and he does not plan to do another.

However, the story of his parents' early marriage, which he wrote as a book, was directed by the Danish film-maker Bille August and released as the film *The Best Intentions (Den Goda Viljan)* in 1992. The six-hour long film was shown on Swedish television but a shortened version was released in the cinemas, and it won the Palme d'Or at the Cannes Film Festival. Bergman is unquestionably one of the greatest directors in the film world, but his work is not universally appreciated. Just because he is Swedish certainly doesn't mean that all Swedes enjoy his films. Nor is his work necessarily representative of Sweden. One of his films, made in the 1950s, was about free love in Sweden. Probably much of the international sex reputation Sweden has can be traced to this type of film.

Many other Swedish directors in the 1960s and 1970s (and today) enjoyed international acclaim. Vilgot Sjöman, Jan Troell and Bo Widerberg worked worldwide on feature films and documentaries.

Today's filmmakers include several who have been successful in Hollywood and others who have chosen to work in Sweden. The recent film *Together*, a story of children growing up in a Swedish commune in the 1970s, from young director Lukas Moodysson was a hit outside Sweden. A few years ago, in the 1990s, films such as *What's Eating Gilbert Grape?* and *My Life as a Dog*, brought acclaim to director Lasse Hallström, while Bo Widerberg's *Med Lust och Fagring Stor*, was nominated for an Oscar in 1996. The English director Colin Nutley, who lives in Sweden, has created several very popular films showing a very Swedish village (actually filmed in Ulricehamm, not far from Göteborg) and some less typically Swedish visitors who come during the summer. Of course, the visitors are also Swedish, but are modern entertainers, and the story of how they fit into the village is very amusing.

Foreign Films

Films from all over the world are enjoyed in Sweden, and you may find that many non-English-language films are released earlier in Sweden than in English speaking countries. There seems to be more of a willingness to watch films from different cultures than in many English-speaking countries, though, of course, Hollywood films are extremely popular in Sweden as well.

Both films and videos in Sweden are shown in the original language, with subtitles (except for children's films), so you won't have to wait until you can speak Swedish to enjoy them. However, the Swedish film industry produces many entertaining films, and it's worth trying these out as soon as your language ability is up to it.

Censorship

There is some state censorship of the film industry, and there is also a rating system, primarily to help parents decide which films are suitable for their children. The ratings are 7, 11 and 15, and they refer to the ages under which children are not allowed to see the film without parental supervision. Films which show too much violence can be censored, or given a higher rating. Unlike in the USA, where violence is rarely considered objectionable but sex is often censored, the Swedish authorities feel that it's less important to censor sex scenes than violence.

TELEVISION AND RADIO

As with film, so with television – a lot of imported programmes are shown in the original language, with Swedish subtitles. There are two main Swedish television channels *(Kanal 1 and TV2)* which are non-commercial. Everyone with a television set pays a licence fee to the state-run Swedish Broadcasting Corporation to support these two channels and Swedish radio. Channels 1 and 2 emphasise cultural, news and educational programming, and the mix of documentaries, live opera and news programmes is sometimes criticised as being too serious and heavy. The standard, however, is generally very high and while these channels import programmes from many countries, they tend to avoid foreign 'light' programming.

The most widely available commercial channel is TV4. Another commercial station, TV3, is often only available to those with a cable connection. Many of the popular American programmes, such as the soap operas and sitcoms, are shown on TV3.

Cable Channels

Many Swedes today enjoy cable television, available either through a cable or through a satellite dish on the roof or in the garden. A basic menu of cable channels is likely to include the English language Eurosport, MTV, CNN and BBC Worldwide. You needn't be without such channels as Discovery, Nickelodeon, FilmNet, or many others, all available in Sweden. Many Swedes watch these programmes as a way of learning what is current in other countries.

Swedish radio offers several alternatives, with programmes in all of the major immigrant languages. Radio Sweden, at 7.38 mHz, broadcasts both international and Swedish news regularly in English. It also offers other English language programmes about Sweden – interesting to listen to if you want to learn more about current events and happenings in Sweden. Several local stations also offer programming in English – check your local paper to see when. The number of commercial stations is growing. In or near a city it is possible to listen to many different types of music and talk programmes.

THE PRESS

Many Swedes prefer to turn to a mix of newspapers and television for their information. The three largest national newspapers are *Expressen* (a tabloid style newspaper with a circulation over 500,000), *Dagens Nyheter* (considered to be an independent liberal broadsheet with a circulation over 400,000) and *Svenska Dagbladet* (considered to be a conservative broadsheet, with a circulation over 200,000). Two other newspapers, *Göteborgs Posten* (circulation 187,000) and *Sydsvenska Dagbladet* (circulation 148,000) are specific to the Göteborg and Malmö regions. In the past, most newspapers were affiliated with political parties, and so had a specific political slant – today, this still holds true of some. Most newspapers have Internet sites. Sweden has taken to the Internet culture faster than most non-English-speaking countries and there is a wealth of websites available, including many with governmental information. The country abbreviation is **.se.**

Freedom of the Press

All newspapers and other press are protected by the Freedom of the Press Act of 1975, which ensures that journalists have the right to protect anonymous sources and have free access to public documents. The Act also establishes procedures for trials concerning freedom of the press, which make it difficult to win financial judgments against journalists. In addition, a special ombudsman governs the press.

Magazines

There are many weekly, monthly and quarterly magazines and journals in Swedish, but for specialist subjects many Swedes turn to foreign magazines. There simply isn't a large enough market to publish specialist magazines only for Swedes. English-language magazines are commonplace in any city, and will probably be available in the libraries of even quite small towns. The same is true of English-language newspapers. British papers are generally available the same day or a day later, while North American or Australasian papers will be between three and eight days old.

BOOKS AND LITERATURE

In addition to being avid newspaper and magazine readers, Swedes buy more books per capita than any other European country. This is in addition to well-funded and utilised libraries. Compulsory education and the long winter evenings have combined to make reading a popular hobby throughout the country. For those who cannot get to their local library there is a system of book-buses and book-boats. These follow a weekly route and it's possible to not only borrow books from them but also order specific books in advance.

Many Swedes buy books from special book clubs through the post. They sometimes specialise in certain subjects, and there are several clubs that offer English-language books.

Bestsellers in English speaking countries are often popular in Sweden, and many Swedes choose to buy these books in their original languages. For a foreigner or a recent immigrant, however, buying Swedish literature in English translation is not always as easy.

Nobel Prize Winners

There are many Swedish Nobel laureates in literature, but perhaps only two of these, Selma Lagerlöf and Pär Lagerkvist are well known outside Sweden. Lagerlöf won the Prize in 1909. She also wrote popular children's tales. The literary trend of the late 19th century celebrated Swedish history and culture, which Lagerlöf and other authors depicted the agrarian lifestyle of days gone in idylls which meant to represent the ideal Swedish lifestyle. This trend was mirrored in musical and artistic creations of the time.

By the early 20th century, during Pär Lagerkvist's (Nobel Prize Laureate in 1951) time, the climate was less positive. His works focus on the themes of existentialism and the struggle between good and evil, with *The Sibyl* and *Barabbas* among his best known works.

Other Literary Figures

The works of well-known author and playwright August Strindberg (1849–1912) are widely available in English. Plays such as *The Father* and *Miss Julie* are performed worldwide. Both Lagerkvist's and Strindberg's works offer an often desperate and bleak view of life; though this ought not to be taken as a general reflection of Swedes!

Proletarian literature first became popular in the 1930s. Authors such as Ivar-Lo Johansson and Harry Martinson wrote about the working classes, often with the theme of social injustice and giving an excellent depiction of their lives of hard work and poverty in the 19th and early 20th centuries. The works of the best-known author of this genre, Vilhelm Moberg (1898–1973), are available in English and have been made into films starring Max von Sydow (another famous Swedish actor) and Liv Ullman. The quartet of books, *The Emigrants*, *The Immigrants*, *The Settlers* and *The Last Letter Home*, tell the story of an impoverished Swedish family's immigration to America.

Few recent Swedish books are available in English. Some authors to look out for are Jan Myrdal, a talented documentarist with sometimes controversial political ideas, and Kerstin Ekman, Sven Delblanc and Jan Guillou, all popular novelists with very different styles.

In the 1990s there has been new interest in Scandinavian literature in the English-speaking world, with Peter Høeg of Denmark (author of *Miss Smilla's Feeling for Snow*) and Jostein Gaarder of Norway (author of *Sophie's World*) paving the way. More of Kerstin Ekman's works have been recently made available in English, and the works of Henning Mankell have become so popular in English that many of his older works are now been translated as well. Another author to look out for is Marianne Fredericksson.

Fortunately, many children's authors have been translated, giving English-speaking children access to the works of Elsa Beskow, Astrid Lindgren's Pippi Longstocking and Emil, and Selma Lagerlöf's wonderfully adventurous Nils. If you have children, these books are a great way to introduce them to some of their new playmates' favourite characters (there are also many spin-off television programmes). Astrid Lindgren's books, and the author herself, are considered by many to be part of Sweden's national treasure. Indeed, during Astrid Lindgren's recent funeral ceremonies, the whole of Sweden mourned and many took to the the streets of Stockholm to pay their last respects to their beloved author.

Chapter Nine

BUSINESS IN SWEDEN

ECONOMY AND INDUSTRY

Sweden has grown, in under a hundred years, from a poor agrarian society to a high-tech and modern industrial and service economy. The traditional exports of Sweden were timber and iron, and both still play a part in the economy today, with engineering products, car and aircraft manufacture and the paper industry all having grown from the forestry and metals industries.

Major Industries

Among the largest industries in Sweden are the engineering and automotive industries. Both Volvo and Saab-Scania are important employers in Sweden, as are Ericsson, ABB, Electrolux and SKF in engineering and manufacturing. Much of the success of these companies is due to strong export performances – the Swedish market is too small to support a large company on its own.

The forestry industry provides jobs for many in the north and, indirectly, for many in the pulp and paper industries in the whole of Sweden. The paper industry alone accounts for 11% of the total industrial value of Sweden. Firms such as Stora, SCA, Tetra-Pak and Mölnlycke work with forest products.

Other natural resources, the metals and iron ore in Sweden, have provided work for miners in northern Sweden for years. The mining industry is in decline, but the Swedish steel industry, after much modernisation and investment, is still successful, exporting 80% of its products.

Other important industries are the telecommunications and computer industry, the chemical industry (with AstraZenecca and Pharmacia as the largest companies) and the arms industry (with both Bofors and such aeronautical companies as Saab as big players). Many Swedes have now found work in service industries, as the recent economic downturn has also hit Sweden and the many Swedes who worked in telecommunications and the IT industries hard.

WORKING CONDITIONS

The historic importance of labour unions in Sweden has meant that Swedish employees have excellent working conditions compared with most countries. The majority of Swedes belong to one of the large unions, such as the LO (over two million members), with mostly blue-collar workers, the TCO, with mostly white-collar workers or SACO/SR, the union for academics. There is also a union for employers, called the Swedish Employers' Confederation (SAF), with over 40,000 member companies.

The unions have worked together for such labour legislation as the Security of Employment Act (1974), the Act on Equality Between Men and Women (1980) and the Co-determination Act (1977) which ensures employee participation in decision making.

The first Act ensures that no employee can be dismissed or demoted unless there is an objective reason for doing so, and that no employee's job description can be changed without consultation with the employee's union. This has meant an increase in job security in general for Swedes, although this has been tested in the recent recession. Other union victories over the past hundred years have resulted in reduced working hours, increased holiday time, the right to leaves of absence for studying or for having a child, and better pay settlements.

Working Hours and Leisure Time

Working hours for most Swedes are between 8 or 9 in the morning and 4 or 5 in the evening. Most work between 35 and 40 hours a week, and overtime is regulated by the Working Hours Act, to a maximum amount in a month and a year. Workers are entitled to a meal break after five hours of work, and must be allowed at least 36 hours of leisure time in every week, usually at the weekends.

By law an employee is entitled to 25 days of paid holiday a year, and there are also 12 public holidays. When a public holiday falls on a Thursday or a Tuesday, the Friday or the Monday are called 'squeeze-days' (klämdager) and many employees work a little extra every day in order to take these days off. These are given in lieu of overtime in many companies. Many Swedes choose to take three or four weeks of their holiday in July, and a company is required to allow four continuous weeks of holiday between June and August, unless there is a collective agreement stating otherwise. Sweden comes close to closing down during July but since joining the European Union more companies are working at least partially throughout the summer.

More labour legislation ensures that if you are too ill to work, your employer is required to pay part of your salary on the second to the thirteenth day of your illness. The first day of illness, called a karensdag, is unpaid to discourage workers ringing in sick for extra time off. After the 13th day the state takes over and pays your sickness benefit. If your child is ill you are entitled to time off to take care of him or her. Parental leave on the birth of a child is granted equally to mothers and fathers, who can share up to 390 days leave of absence at 80% of pay, with a further 90 days at a fixed rate.

Employment Contracts

Contracts are legally binding in Sweden, whether written or verbal, and you should receive written notification of your terms and conditions of employment within a month of starting work. You are protected against unfair dismissal, and have certain entitlements in any permanent job. The exception is if your contract stipulates that it is a temporary contract, with fewer rights. Pay is either as a salary, paid weekly or monthly, or as a wage, paid depending on how many hours you have worked in a given period. There should be a health and safety representative at every firm employing more than five people, and employees are insured by law against work injury.

SWEDES AT WORK

Swedes have a strong work ethic, but guard their private time fiercely. This doesn't mean they will never work overtime, just that they will need to be convinced there is a good reason for it. Their family life is very important to them, and many will have arrangements with child-carers that they do not want to upset. When you work with Swedish colleagues you should respect the work hours they keep. They will be punctual in both arriving and leaving and that, a Swede will tell you, is how it should be. By the same token, work is not often taken home, and business entertaining will generally not be in private homes.

Swedish business structures generally tend to be flat, rather than hierarchical, as in the pyramid structures of many American and British firms. Of course the managing director is the boss, but he (or she) will usually be accessible for all employees, and relations

Many Swedes work in modern office blocks, like the one to the left of this picture. In the centre, Göteborg's new opera house is trying to revitalise a harbour front which has suffered from the decline in the shipping industries.

between different job levels are often open and informal. The workplace itself will often feel quite informal, with casual dress and decor common. Swedes like to feel comfortable and happy at work, and many firms have sports clubs and special interest groups who meet at lunch-time or after work. It's not unusual for workers to take a company sponsored long weekend skiing in the mountains, or in another city, all together. The employers consider it a team building exercise, and it's an enjoyable way to get to know your colleagues better.

As with Swedes at school and at play, consensus is important in business life. It's better to reach a solution through cooperation, even if it takes longer, than through an independent decision handed down. In keeping with their national character, Swedish employees downplay their achievements and don't look for extra credit for work well done.

The qualities which characterise the Swedes in other areas, such as caution, pragmatism, efficiency and quietness, are all evident in the way a Swede conducts business.

FINDING WORK AS AN IMMIGRANT

In recent years, the unemployment rate has been high for Swedes and immigrant unemployment has been higher still. If you can build on any Swedish contacts in your field before you move you will improve your chances of finding work. Otherwise, if you have not been transferred by your home company to Sweden, your job search will start at the *Arbetsförmedlingen* (Job Centre). Any immigrant who is attending SFI language classes can also ask the SFI consultant for help with the *Arbetsförmedlingen* system. Each Job Centre has several consultants, who will interview you to try to place you in the right job. In cities the Job Centres may handle only one type of industry, so you should check that you are in the right place for what you want to do.

Once you have completed the forms and your interview, you can receive help with applying for jobs and for training and courses. If you are entitled to unemployment benefit you are required to attend the Job Centre to collect it. Job vacancies are advertised on the job centre's website at www.ams.se. After a certain period of unemployment you may be entitled to job-hunting classes, covering interview skills, letter-writing skills, and learning how to target yourself. Your consultant can help you find out about these options.

Aside from the Job Centres, many employers place advertisements in the local newspapers. It's worth checking the small adverts, particularly if you are interested in casual work, as many private employers advertise there. If you want to target a certain type of company, a speculative letter to companies found in the yellow pages of the telephone directory, followed up by a telephone call, can work well. You don't necessarily need to write the initial letter in Swedish (English is respected as a business language) but you ought to have

155

enough Swedish to follow up on the phone, even if it's fairly halting.

If you are under 25, you should look into special practical places, where the government pays you a salary while you gain experience in working for a firm. The firms often take on the 'practice workers' as permanent employees at the end of the six-month placement.

Qualifications

A drawback to finding work in Sweden, aside from casual work, is that many professions require Swedish qualifications and so you may have to retrain. Most jobs in Sweden require specific qualifications, and while in other countries a general university degree will open doors to many careers, in Sweden you are expected to have specific training. Another drawback is that you will need excellent Swedish in many jobs, and your proficiency in English will not always be a significant advantage to an employer who may have many Swedish employees with excellent command of English.

Any preparation you do in advance, such as taking a TEFL (Teaching English as Foreign Language) certificate, building up contacts, or finishing a professional qualification, will help you immensely. You might also like to look into having any professional qualifications translated into the Swedish equivalents. The AMS should be able to advise on this.

GOOD POSSIBILITIES FOR WORK AND BUSINESSES

Many immigrants work as foreign language teachers in private and adult education schools (to work in the Swedish school system you will need a full teaching qualification from Sweden or another European Union country), in restaurants and pubs, and in casual jobs at least initially. There are a lot of English language teaching opportunities, through both business English centres and evening classes, but there are a lot of well established teachers who new arrivals will have to compete with. Once you start getting work you will gradually be able to build up your hours, especially if the school realises that you are settling in Sweden. The better qualified you are (either with a TEFL certificate or in business in your home country) the better the pay and conditions you will get, so it's worth thinking about getting some experience before moving to Sweden.

Looking for restaurant work is often best in person. Turn up at the place you want to work and see if they need help. Around Easter is an excellent time to start in many areas, because many restaurants have outside serving areas open only in the summer months, and need to hire extra staff for the summer. There are many English style pubs and restaurants, some of which are owned by expatriate Brits, Irish, Australians or Americans. The language spoken at work is sometimes English and it's a good idea to target these places first.

Starting Your Own Business

If you're not keen on casual work or teaching, and can't get work through any contacts, it's worth looking into starting your own business. A surprisingly high number of immigrants do this, either importing goods from their own countries or offering services such as translation.

Many evening class centres offer courses on starting your own business (called *Starta eget* – start your own), and if your Swedish is up to it they can offer a lot of useful advice. If you are interested in starting an import-export business, you may like to ask the Swedish Trade Council (at www.swedishtrade.com) for advice. They can provide useful information about customs, importing regulations and trade links with foreign firms.

All new companies in Sweden must register with the Register of Companies, the tax office and the social security office. Employees' rights are strictly regulated and you should make certain that you are up to date with these before employing extra staff. SAF, the trade union for employers, can help you with information about this, as can the Confederation of Swedish Enterprise at www.svensktnaringsliv.se/index_english.asp or the Invest in Sweden Agency at www.isa.se. You can usually raise finance, even for a foreign company, through a Swedish bank. There are also several grants and special loans available to business-people starting their own companies, and it's worthwhile consulting the relevant development funds, or your local Job Centre to find out about these. You can also get information from the local authorities *(länsstyrelsen)* or your local tax office.

— Chapter Ten —

SETTLING IN SWEDEN

BEFORE YOU MOVE

The first thing to sort out before you move is your visa, or permission to stay in Sweden. If your company is transferring you, they should sort this out for you.

If you are a European Union citizen you have the right to a work permit in Sweden. You may stay in the country for three months while you look for work. To obtain a residence permit, you must present your passport and proof of your employment at the local police station. They will grant you a residence permit for the period of employment, or for five years if the employment is permanent. Once you are working in Sweden with a residence permit, your spouse or partner and any children under 21 or elderly parents who are your dependants may also apply for residence permits, even if they are not EU citizens.

European Union citizens who want to live in Sweden without working can also apply to the police for a residence permit, but must have proof that they can support themselves without state assistance. Usually proof of bank deposits or else a guarantee from another person that they will support you is enough. Students can also apply for residence permits, as long as they can prove they can support themselves, as can EU pensioners.

Immigration Without European Union Membership

If you are not an EU national you will find it much more difficult. Immigration controls are very strict, and unless you have a family connection or a strong business connection it is unlikely you will be able to move. The family connection can be with a Swedish resident, rather than a Swedish citizen. Dependent children (under 21), dependent parents and spouses are the most likely to be admitted.

If you are in a relationship with a Swedish citizen (which does not have to be marriage), you can apply for a residence permit as a common law spouse. Application should be made from outside of Sweden, at the Swedish embassy or consulate in your country. Both you and your partner will be asked to fill out forms and will be interviewed separately, the Swede at his or her local police station and you at the embassy. A residence permit will normally be granted for six months, though it is renewable after another interview at your local police station. You can continue applying for the six-monthly permits, or apply for a permanent permit. If you are not granted a permanent one you will normally receive another six-month permit. In every case, allow at least six to eight weeks for your application to be processed by the embassy or consulate.

WHAT TO TAKE

Now that you are ready to go, what should you take with you? We've already looked at what clothes and furniture you may like to take.

Winter sports equipment, a shortwave radio and extra camera film (it's expensive in Sweden) have all been useful for other immigrants. When bringing electrical appliances, be sure of their compatibility with Swedish circuits – Swedish electricity is 220 volts, and plugs usually have two round prongs; you'll find it easier to buy converters and adaptors in your home country before you come.

On a personal level, you may like to pack an extra supply of English reading material (widely available but not cheap in Sweden) and favourite foods from your own country. Order any magazine or newspaper subscriptions that you'd like before you move if possible. You are allowed to import up to three months' worth of medicine for personal use only. Doing this will buy you time to find out which Swedish equivalent works for you. If you drink alcohol, import the maximum allowed from your part of the world.

There are no restrictions on the amount of foreign currency you can import into Sweden. It is a good idea to take all of your important documentation with you, such as your birth certificates, any educational certificates and an international driver's licence, and to set up a power of attorney in your home country if you are leaving a business or a house behind you.

WHAT NOT TO TAKE

Don't bother to pack televisions, video recorders or answerphones – they will most likely not be compatible with the Swedish ones. If you want to bring video cassettes from the United States, however, you will have to bring your video recorder with you because the cassettes are not compatible with the Swedish PAL system. You won't be able to record on a foreign VCR but you may be able to play back. You may not be able to play American DVDs on a Swedish DVD player, either, because of territorial restrictions. Remember, also, that you do not need to take your refrigerator, freezer or oven with you; Swedes leave these behind when they move away, so there will already be one in your new home.

161

Don't take fresh meats, dairy produce or eggs without permission, or illegal drugs and restricted animal products, such as ivory. If in doubt check with the embassy first.

It is expensive to import your car to Sweden, especially if you plan to sell it within a year or if it is a new model. To register it you are required to ensure it is up to Swedish environmental standards, and if you sell the car within a year you will have to pay import duties on it. You may find it easier to buy a Swedish car after you move. Again, the embassy can help you with the specific regulations.

PETS

If you are moving to Sweden temporarily, consider finding a short-term home for your pet rather than taking it with you. Animal immigration regulations are strict and your pet may have to be quarantined at one of the quarantine stations in Stenungsund, Sollefteå, Furuland and Vallentuna. But if you can't bear to be separated, you need to obtain an import permit, issued by the National Board for Agriculture. This involves your vet granting your dog or cat an Export Health Certificate (in your home country), identifying your pet with a tattoo or an implanted microchip and treating your pet against internal parasites several weeks before you move. Write to: The National Board of Agriculture, Division of Contagious Diseases, 551 82 Jönköping, Sweden, for the leaflet they produce on importing dogs and cats to Sweden.

HOUSING

The standard of housing in Sweden is very high, with most homes having central heating, good insulation and modern plumbing. Just over half of Swedes live in a house, with the rest living in apartments. Most apartments are housed in blocks of flats, rather than in converted houses. Houses are commonly either terraced (row) houses or else detached houses. The traditional wooden houses are back in fashion after many years of modern designs, though in all homes natural sunlight and clean interiors add the feel of simplicity that is typical of Swedish design.

Most Swedish homes will include a fridge, a freezer and a washing machine. Practical work areas and storage spaces are a priority. Most flats will have a specific storage area either attached to the flat or else in the basement of the block, and a special laundry room. With good insulation and double, triple or sometimes quadruple glazed windows, there is no need to draw the curtains at night to keep away the cold and few Swedes do. Most homes are furnished comfortably but in style. Swedes appreciate good design and enjoy their rural roots, which is evident in their style of interior design. You will often see traditional elements such as wooden *köksoffor* (kitchen benches), folk-painted brooms and sheaves of dried flowers within a very modern design. Swedes love nature, so their homes are often filled with houseplants.

Most households (over 60%) in Sweden are made up of just one or two people, with many young adults leaving home early and fewer elderly people moving in with their extended families. Many communities of flats and rowhouses are built around a playground area and common buildings for laundry facilities and bicycle storage. In spite of this, in urban areas it's not unusual for neighbours not to know each other, although many say they would welcome friendly neighbours.

163

Finding a Home

There are three main ways of finding a home in Sweden; renting a flat, partly buying a flat or a house (paying an initial deposit *(insats)* and then a monthly rent *(hyran)*, or buying a house outright. About 40% of all homes are rented, and tenants are protected under Swedish law against unfair rent increases. The law also ensures that you may not be charged significantly more for your flat than for a similar one in the same building. The rent generally includes heating and maintenance, including redecorating.

To rent a flat you can either go through a private agency, or *bostadsföretag*, through a public housing company or sublet from the owner or first tenant (a sublet flat is called an *andrahand* – second-hand flat). You can find the private agencies in the telephone book, but remember they may charge a fee. Nearly half of all rented accommodation in Sweden is owned by the public housing companies.

These blocks of apartments offer a green common area between them. Places for children to play and for everyone to relax are considered important for flat-dwellers.

You may have to put your name on a waiting list to get a flat in a certain area, but they will be able to find you something. The sublet flats are advertised in the local papers and are easy to find. You will have to sign a contract for a fixed amount of time for a sublet, and some flats have restrictions on how long they can be sublet for. It used to be impossible to rent a house but with the current flat housing market some owners are renting rather than selling – check the newspapers or an estate agent *(fastigshetsmäklare)*.

To buy a flat or house, go through the realty agents. You can find them in the yellow pages of the telephone directory called Gula Sidorna in Sweden. The yellow pages are also online at www.gulasidorna.se, with information in English. You can find most of the real estate agents online as well. If you buy a flat or a house which includes use of common areas (i.e. laundry areas, common gardens, etc.) you will have to pay a deposit to actually buy the property, but still pay a monthly rent to cover maintenance and upkeep on the building (for a flat) and/or the common areas. You will also often sign an agreement that restricts what you can do with your property, usually concerning renting it out, using it for business, or renovating it. If you buy a house outright you do not have to pay rent but you are, of course, solely responsible for the building and grounds.

Note that Swedes are safety conscious in the home and many install smoke alarms and security alarms to guard against accidents and break-ins.

GENERAL INFORMATION

Swedish time is one hour ahead of Greenwich Mean Time, and changes in summertime to be two hours ahead of Greenwich Mean Time. The summertime change is coordinated with the rest of the European Union, so that when it is 1:00 p.m. in London, it is always 2:00 p.m. in Sweden. (Remember that Swedes tell time by the 24-hour clock, using 1400 instead of 2:00 p.m.)

All measurements are in the metric system, including temperature

(Celsius), weights (kilograms and grams), liquids (litres) and distances (kilometres and metres). However, there is one extra measurement which is an old Nordic one. Ten kilometres is often referred to as a mile *(en mil)* – or a 'Swedish mile' in English. For this reason, if you talk about the English or American mile, you should call it the English mile or the American mile to differentiate.

Registering

If you plan to live in Sweden for any length of time you must register with the authorities. To do this, take your passport with your work/ resident permit information to the tax authorities, and be ready to fill out some forms. The clerks there will help you if your Swedish is still weak or nonexistent. You must register with both the local and social insurance authorities. They will issue you with a personal number *(personnummer)* which is vital for living in Sweden – you quote it for work, for your bank, at the doctor's, and when using a credit card in many shops. You will need this number before you can register for Swedish language lessons or any social benefits.

The number will consist of six digits (your date of birth), a dash, and then four digits which are your personal number and differentiate you from others with the same birth date. For example, someone born on April 1, 1996, might have the number 960401-2938. The second to last digit is even for females and odd for males.

Banks and Money

The Swedish currency is the crown, called *krona* (plural *kronor*) in Swedish, and *öre*. Two abbreviations often used are 'SEK,' placed in front of the number, or 'Kr' placed afterwards. The money system is metric, with 100 *öre* making up a crown, although the smallest coin is for 50 *öre*, with other coins being 1 crown, 5 crown and 10 crown. Notes are in denominations of 20, 50, 100, 500, 1000 and 10,000 crowns. Some larger shops in tourist areas will accept German marks, British sterling and American dollars as payment as well. Sweden is one of the countries which has adopted a 'wait-and-see' attitude to the euro, although it is likely to be acceptable as payment where foreign currencies are, when the EU issues coins and paper money. However, there will be a national referendum in September 2003 on whether they should also adopt the euro currency.

If you are exchanging money in Sweden one of the best rates of exchange is at the Forex (foreign exchange) counters in the larger cities. If you keep your receipt you will be able to exchange your Swedish currency back into your home currency without paying a commission at any Forex counter. You may not export more than SEK6,000 in Swedish currency. It is relatively simple to transfer money from an overseas bank to a Swedish one, and can take as little as a day from either Britain or the US, but you will be charged both a transfer and a currency exchange fee. If you can, carry as much money as you will want with you when you move, preferably in travellers' cheques, for depositing into your bank account.

Opening a bank account is easy, but you will need a personal number to do it. There are different types of accounts and the staff at the bank should be able to advise you on which is best for you. Transfer of money between accounts at Swedish banks is simple and fast and most bills are paid by bank transfer. You do this by filling out bank transfer forms with the accounts payable, and sending the forms to your bank. When the funds have been transferred your bank sends notification to the payee. This system replaces cheques for most Swedes, and cheques are not widely used. Note that it is difficult to deposit a foreign cheque into a Swedish bank; the length of time it takes and the fee charged make it not worthwhile.

Most bank accounts will issue you with a cash machine card, so that you can obtain money from a cash machine in the wall of the bank after hours, and you may also find an account card *(kontokort)* useful. This card works like a credit card when paying for goods and services but the money is transferred directly out of your account. In Sweden it is normal for your salary to be paid directly into your bank account.

167

Your pay packet will consist of a pay advice slip, letting you know how much has been deposited into your account.

As in many countries, internet banking has become very popular and many Swedes run their accounts online.

Taxation

The Swedish taxation system works on a pay as you earn basis, so your pay slip will already have income tax deducted from it. Your bank will also deduct taxes from the interest you earn as necessary. Swedish taxes are progressive, so you will pay more as you earn more, but there is a maximum of 50%, and the average payment is 31%. Indirect taxation is high compared with many other countries, with a value-added tax *(MOMS)* of 25% on most goods and services. Food has a lower MOMS rating, while alcohol has a higher one. Depending on what country you come from, and how long you intend to stay in Sweden, you should check that you will have home tax relief because of paying tax in Sweden. Many countries have double tax agreements (among them the UK and the US) and many European countries will also have social security agreements, so that you can apply social security payments made in Sweden to your home country's system.

Although the taxes may seem high, remember that you are entitled to a range of benefits in exchange for them. Several which result in financial payouts are child benefit, parental leave and housing benefit. If you earn under a certain amount you can apply for housing benefit to help pay your rent. You can also claim child benefit for each child, and can take paid time off work after the birth of a child. For any of these you must be registered with the tax authorities for a certain time before you are eligible. Check with them or with the local Immigrant Bureau to find out which you can apply for.

Communications

The Swedish postal system is very efficient, if expensive. Post offices are open 9:30 a.m. to 6:00 p.m. weekdays and from 10:00 a.m. to 1:00

p.m. on Saturdays. There is one postal delivery a day on weekdays, with none on weekends. All Swedish addresses include a five digit postal code, which will speed up your post. If you live in a block of flats your address may be the same as the other five flats in your block. People writing to you should put your full name on the letter, and you should put your name on the door of your flat so that the postal worker can find you. The post office will also send telegrams and faxes for you, and you can vote, receive your pay (if you receive a *postgirot* payslip rather than the pay going directly into your account) and benefits and collect parcels at the post office.

Most Swedish homes have a telephone. The emergency services telephone number is 90 000, and you will need to be able to tell the operator what has happened, which emergency service you need, and where you are calling from. Don't panic if you can't speak Swedish; operators will do their best in English. When you sign up for a telephone you will need to pay a connection charge and then a quarterly account. You can request an itemised account if you want. The telephone directories are comprehensive, and include residential, business, municipal services and regional services sections. There are usually detailed local maps at the beginning of the directory, and the yellow pages *(gula sidorna)* list businesses by category.

The largest telephone company, although state owned, works as a private corporation and the market is now open for other companies. Competition for both residential and business customers in recent years has driven down telephone bills markedly. At the time of writing there were over 13 companies competing for business in the Gothenburg area, offering varied levels of services. It's worth looking into these companies for cheaper long distance and overseas calls, although with many of them you will have to telephone abroad often to see a substantial saving.

If you are phoning from a phone box you can use coins or else a disposable phone card (available at newsagents and kiosks). Some phones will take credit cards, but they are not as common as in some countries. There are no collect calls within Sweden, although you can make collect calls overseas through your home operator by dialling 020-79 first. The code for overseas calls is 009; for operator assistance call 0019 and for directory assistance call 07975. Numbers starting with 020 are freephone calls. The international country code is 46.

TRANSPORT

Because Sweden is so sparsely populated many Swedes drive private cars to get around. However, public transport between cities and towns and within urban areas is very good, with a bus system operating in most areas. Stockholm also has a subway system and Gothenburg and Norrköping still enjoy trams (streetcars).

Cross Country Travel

For long distances, the Swedish national railways (SJ, which stands for *Statens Järnvägar*) run regional, intercity and express trains. Larger stations will have touch-sensitive maps where you can get travel information and ticket prices in English, otherwise the ticket sellers will usually have some English themselves. The trains are comfortable and punctual, though can be expensive. On night trains you can book a sleeper (with a couchette).

The coach system means that smaller towns and villages not on the railroads are accessible, and the tickets are generally cheaper than train tickets. The coaches stop more often, and some are request stops only, which means you need to look out for your stop and ask the driver for it before you get there. The domestic air service is less frequently used (except by businesspeople) but useful for trips the length of the country which otherwise are extremely long. Scandinavian Airline System (SAS) is the national airline (it's also the national airline for the other Scandinavian countries) and flies hourly between Stockholm and Gothenburg, with regular flights throughout the rest of Sweden. There are sometimes very cheap deals for passengers under 26, or stand-by on the last flight of the night.

If you choose to drive long distances you may notice on road maps that there are a lot of lakes and bays to cross without bridges. These are served by regular car ferries, which are sometimes free (considered part of the road) and sometimes cost money (usually if you have a choice of going around and save time by taking the ferry). Larger ferries between the mainland and Scandinavian islands do cost money, and often need to be booked in advanced, particularly in the summer months.

Local public transport includes buses, trams, trains and ferries again, particularly in the Stockholm and Gothenburg areas. In many cities and towns you can buy a season ticket for a day, a week, a month or a year for a particular area or route – worthwhile if you commute to work by public transport. In addition, taxis in cities are plentiful, as strict drink driving rules mean that few Swedes drive for an evening out on the town, and not expensive if shared between several people.

Driving in Sweden
If you plan to drive in Sweden you need your full licence, but it is useful to have an international driving licence as well. European Union licences are accepted however long you live in Sweden, but any other licence needs to be replaced by a Swedish one within a year of registering yourself as resident in Sweden. It used to be possible to exchange North American and Antipodean licences directly for a Swedish licence, but no longer. To obtain a Swedish licence you will need to pass a written test (which you can take in English), a driving test (with a manual transmission) and a winter driving test (in which you drive on ice and your winter driving skills especially your turning and stopping skills – are assessed). You must be at least 18 years old to drive a car in Sweden.

Swedes drive on the right, and keep car headlamps on at all times. Seatbelts are required front and back, and children under 7 should be in harnesses or child-seats. Remember that safety is paramount in Sweden. Drink driving rules are very strict, and you can be stopped at random and asked to take a breathalyser test. The blood alcohol limit is 0.02%, and you are likely to receive a fine, lose your licence and face possible imprisonment if you are over the limit, so don't drink and drive.

The roads are generally uncrowded, except in the cities. The speed limits are low for Europe; 110 km/h on motorways; 90 km/h on larger roads; and 70 or 50 km/h in built up areas and in towns. Watch out for both pedestrians and cyclists (there are more on Swedish roads than you may be used to) and also for wild animals in rural areas. One encounter with a moose is likely to be one more than your car can handle, and both reindeer and elk wander across roads from time to time. There are usually signs to warn you.

In the winter you will need winter tyres which have deeper treads and sometimes studs, especially in the north. You are not allowed to keep these on your car in the summertime, and a date is set every spring after which you cannot drive with them on your car (usually April 1 or May 1, depending on the region and the severity of the winter). They are allowed again after another date in the autumn, also sct annually. Many petrol stations operate automatic pumps, where you deposit notes or a credit card into the pump to make it work. There are of course staffed self service stations as well.

If you choose to buy a car in Sweden you need to register it in your name, pay a road tax and have the car inspected annually. You are required by law to have third party insurance for it. For more information about the details of this and for obtaining a driving licence, contact the traffic authority in your municipality (called TSV, or *Trafiksäkerhetsverket*).

Bicycles

For an often cold and snowy country, Swedes cycle a lot. This is perhaps not surprising, when you remember how much the average Swede enjoys being outdoors, and cares about the environment. Cycling in Swedish cities is made much easier by excellent cycle paths, often separated from car traffic, and with special traffic lights for cycle traffic. There are many long distance cycle paths linking towns and cities the length of Sweden.

You can buy decent second hand cycles through adverts in the papers or at bicycle shops. Buy a good lock at the same time and lamps, which are required after dusk. Reflectors are also required, but most bikes will come equipped with them. Helmets, baskets, panniers and a bell to warn pedestrians of your approach are other useful purchases.

Many of the bicycle paths can also be used by mopeds, which are popular among the youngsters. You can drive a moped from the age of 15 in Sweden, and a helmet is required for it. They are not very fast, but can use cycle paths and get you about easier than a bicycle can if you aren't fit. Motorcycles must use the ordinary roads, meant for cars. Motorcyclists need a special licence (for which they must be over 18) and are required to wear helmets as well. However, you can drive a 125cc light motorcycle from the age of 16 but a special licence is required.

HEALTHCARE

If you need emergency healthcare in Sweden, you can go to the emergency department of any hospital. As long as you are registered in the Swedish social system you need only give your personal number to be treated. For regular medical care, however, you should make an appointment to see the duty doctor at the local health centre *(Vårdcentral)* when you feel ill. You can often get an immediate appointment if it is urgent, but for a real emergency you should always go to the hospital. Sweden has recently introduced the system of 'family doctors,' similar to the British general practitioner system, whereby you can register with one doctor who you see initially for any complaint or worry. He or she can then refer you further to a specialist if necessary. As a new system this is still under review – many people favour the idea as it leads to more personalised service, but others object to it because they think it might lead to inefficiency and lower standards of health care. Although health care is heavily subsidised in Sweden, you do need to pay a fee for a doctor's appointment.

The exception to paying a fee is if you need to see a midwife, in the Mother's Health Care Centre *(Mödrarvårdscentralen)*. At this centre you can receive advice and prescriptions for contraception and pre and postnatal care. You will need to go to the centre in your area; check the municipal pages of the phone directory for information. Contraception is readily available in Sweden and encouraged, both to prevent unwanted pregnancies and, in some cases, to prevent diseases like AIDS spreading. Abortion is a right in Sweden and is free on request up until the end of the 18th week of pregnancy. There is no stigma attached to using contraception, abortion or choosing to have a child out of wedlock.

Pharmacies

Should you get a prescription from your doctor or midwife, you will need to visit the chemist, or drug store, or pharmacy, which is called *Apoteket* in Sweden. This is a monopoly so if you want medicines you

174

must buy them here. They also sell shampoos, soaps, toothpastes and other similar items, but these are also sold in supermarkets and often are cheaper there. To buy something at an *Apoteket* you must take a number when you go in, and then wait for it to be called. Prescriptions are often filled while you wait, and are subsidised by the state so are not too expensive. If you need to buy a lot of a medicine (for example, for an ongoing condition), you can obtain a card to show how much you have spent on medicine. Once you have spent over a certain amount within a calendar year, all other medicine you need for your personal use will be free that year. You can include the cost of medical treatment on your 'high paying' card as well.

If you don't have a prescription, you follow the same procedure and ask the chemist for advice. They have excellent training and you can often avoid paying to see a doctor if you have a common complaint, as they can provide you with the cure. However, many drugs which do not require a prescription elsewhere are regulated in Sweden. For example, strong cough medicines which you can buy over the counter in the United States, Australia and the United Kingdom are only available on prescription in Sweden. Antibiotics which are widely available in Asia are also regulated.

Seeing a dentist in Sweden is similar to most other countries; you ring up a dentist and ask for an appointment. Dental treatment is also heavily subsidised and there is a set fee per hour (currently SEK660). For emergencies you can contact the emergency out-of-hours dentist on duty. This service is usually only available in large cities, listed in the telephone directory.

It is worth noting that children up to the age of 19 receive free healthcare, dental treatment and eye checkups, as well as subsidised eyeglasses if needed.

EDUCATION

Formal schooling for Swedish children begins when they are 6, and if you have children between the ages of 6 and 16 they are required by law to attend school. However, many Swedish children start earlier, by going to a childcare centre where the carers combine play and learning, and then often continue on to either a preschool *(förskola)* or a play-school *(lekskola)* before starting school. Often this is because both parents work, but it is considered an advantage and helps children get a start on socialising with other children and gaining some independence away from their parents. As of January 2003 all children age four and five have the right to a free preschool place. They can also stay in their childcare centres, where the cost to the parents is limited by a 'max tax' scheme (called *maxtaxa*). Parents pay according to their income but never more than a fixed (low) level per month.

Until recently, compulsory schooling was broken up into three divisions of three years each – primary school *(lågstadiet)*, middle school *(mellanstadiet)* and high school *(högstadiet)*. There are still nine years of compulsory schooling but the traditional divisions have gone and children are now examined after five years and again on completion of the ninth year. This educational reform began in the 1995–1996 school year and, again, is under review.

The majority of children attend state comprehensive schools for their compulsory schooling. There are very few private schools and home schooling is not allowed. However, those parents who choose to send their children to private schools can now receive a government voucher as part payment of the fees, to help them. There are several international schools, teaching in English or other foreign languages, in the larger cities, as well as religious schools. For children who are particularly talented in sport, or music, there are several specialised schools with restricted admission where they will study the ordinary school subjects but have their studies scheduled around extra time for practices, games and recitals.

Certain subjects are compulsory in Swedish schools, among them mathematics, Swedish, English, social studies (including geography, history and religion), science (including biology, chemistry and physics) and physical education. Both boys and girls learn home economics and handicraft so that boys can sew and girls can carve wood. In addition there are many elective subjects, such as other foreign languages, of which German is the most popular.

The school year is broken up into two semesters, with Christmas and summer holidays in between them. The autumn semester starts earlier than in most European countries, in late August, breaks usually in late October/early November and ends at Christmas time. The spring semester breaks twice – once for a 'sports holiday' in February, and once at Easter. The actual dates of the holidays are staggered throughout different school areas, so that not all school children are on holiday at once, except in the summer and Christmas holidays. Schools are in session from early morning to mid-afternoon, Monday to Friday.

After finishing compulsory schooling, usually at the age of 15 or 16, over 95% of all students continue on to further education through a *gymnasium*. At this point in time students specialise and can choose vocational, technical or academic lines, depending on where their interests lie. For some academic lines students will need high marks from their final years in school. It is possible to study an international curriculum, leading to A-Levels, SATs or the International Baccalaureate.

Books, lunches and transport to and from school are provided free of charge throughout school and gymnasium, and dress code and discipline is relaxed, making for a generally friendly and pleasant atmosphere. Competition is not emphasised in Swedish schools as much as cooperation in learning, and this aspect of Swedish education has its critics who say that the system discourages high achievers. The natural counter-argument is that cooperation fosters learning. This argument leads to several often debated subjects, such as that of grades and standardised tests, and whether children should be graded at all.

Another such subject is whether the role of a teacher is to hand down knowledge or lead students to discovering knowledge themselves. The Swedish educational system is now working to balance the newer ideas of cooperative teaching with the call for back-to-basics teaching, so that students will benefit by receiving the best of both systems.

Students who want to study further after gymnasium can choose one of over 30 universities and places of higher education, and 38% do go on to further study. Subjects studied range again from vocational through to academic. Tuition is free, but students pay for their own board, lodging and books, often through a government sponsored student loan system. Most courses last four years, though it depends on the courses, and most courses are modular, similar to the American college system.

Adult Education

There is ample provision in Sweden for adults who want to continue to study, even if they did not choose to continue to higher education directly from school. The Adult Education system *(Komvux* for short) offers courses both in subjects which can build towards university entrance and in vocational subjects for training towards a different career. These courses carry no course fee, and students can apply for study grants to compensate for lost income. Note that you cannot apply for these grants before you have been resident for two years in Sweden. In addition to the municipal and state run adult education courses, there are many private educational centres offering different courses. Charges vary, but are often quite inexpensive, depending on the subject.

Immigrants are entitled to free Swedish language instruction, and children of immigrants can receive both extra Swedish language instruction for school work as well as extra lessons in their native language, to encourage them to become bilingual. (See Chapter Five for more details.)

CRIME AND THE POLICE

The crime rate in Sweden generally is very low, with the most common offence being drink driving (an effect of the very strict laws). Violent crime is on the increase in Sweden, as in many countries, but gun control is stringent, and most people do not feel their personal security is threatened. If you do need to report a crime, ring 90 000, the general emergency number, and ask for *polislarm* (police alarm).

If you are arrested you should inform your embassy or consulate immediately. You can be detained for up to 12 hours, and then for a further day after orders from a prosecutor. Everyone is entitled to legal representation in Sweden; the court will appoint a representative for you, or you can request a specific one. There is an extensive legal aid system, and you can request an hour of discounted legal advice from any lawyer.

Sentencing for criminal offences is generally geared toward rehabilitation rather than simple punishment and there is no death penalty in Sweden. The harshest sentence a criminal can receive is lifetime imprisonment but in practice this generally means between 7 and 16 years. For lesser crimes, sentences can include fines, community service, between 14 days to 16 years imprisonment, or a combination of these.

Prisoners are offered training, particularly vocational and social, and help in fighting alcohol or drug dependency, to ensure that they can rejoin society when they are released. Some prisoners are also granted leaves without supervision to help them prepare themselves for freedom, while others, particularly young offenders, are taken on character building trips in the countryside. Swedes debate whether these measures should be allowed, or whether correctional care should be stricter.

CITIZENSHIP

When you have lived in Sweden for two years, you are eligible to vote in local elections. Once you have lived in Sweden for five years, you can apply for Swedish citizenship. The Swedish authorities recognise only one citizenship, so if you become a Swedish citizen you will have to give up your previous citizenship.

There are three ways of becoming a Swedish citizen; through birth, through naturalisation, and through application. Any child born to a Swedish mother, or to a Swedish father who is married to the child's mother, is entitled to Swedish citizenship. If the child's parents are unmarried, and the father is Swedish, the child can become entitled to citizenship if the parents subsequently marry.

To become a citizen through naturalisation, you must have lived in Sweden for five years (or two years if you are from one of the other Nordic countries), be over 18 and have no criminal record. It's worth knowing that there is a faster way – through application; if you have lived in Sweden since you were 16 continuously, and are between 21 and 23-years-old. Former Swedish citizens can be granted citizenship again after two years of residency, on application.

COMBATING CULTURE SHOCK IN SWEDEN

When moving to any new culture people often find that the first few months are easier than the next four to six. You'll be busy settling in, finding places to frequent, meeting new friends, and Sweden will seem exotic to you. Take advantage of these first few months to get to know the Swedish way of life a bit better.

The second stage of culture shock takes place when you realise that you are actually living in Sweden and may be there for some time. Anything that you dislike is magnified now, and you're likely to start comparing everything with the way things are back home. (When you start thinking that people pushing on the morning bus commute are actually more polite back home, then you know you're suffering from the second stage!) You seem to have reached a plateau in language learning, so that you can almost get by but don't feel you'll ever really be conversant in Swedish.

Some people think it's a good idea to plan a holiday home within three months. Others think you might suffer even more by comparing your home, where your friends are (and you're on holiday), with Sweden, where you are going through culture shock and working. A good compromise is to invite family or friends to come visit you. You'll relive your first exciting months in Sweden by showing your friends around, making you feel more positive about the place.

The third big stage of culture shock is acculturatisation – which comes gradually. Even while you are still criticising the weather or the food, you will come to accept the Swedish way of life. Your language will improve without your noticing it, and you will make real Swedish friends. If you do eventually go back home you'll find yourself affected by Swedish values and 'the Swedish way' of doing things.

It is possible to understand and live the Swedish way without abandoning your own culture, and you can do this by socializing with other immigrants, and travelling home regularly. At the same time you may start to disapprove of certain things in your home country (after all, you've picked up the Swedish value system). But don't disapprove when you're with your old friends and family – they haven't lived through the same culture shock, and may not appreciate hearing your new ideas. Be sensitive to this, so that you don't lose your connections with your home country.

If you have recently moved to Sweden, you may be wondering just how long this adjustment will take. As you've probably guessed, there are no rules about this. From purely personal experience I have found that people in full time work similar to their work at home adjust quickest, while children in Swedish schools also help families to adjust. It took most immigrants I knew between six and eight months to feel at home in Sweden, and perhaps another four to six months to settle into the Swedish way of life. People who were transferred to Sweden for work, and knew they would only be in Sweden for a year or two, often maintained the best attitude towards the differences. If you find it very difficult to adjust, try pretending that you will only be in Sweden a short time, so you will take the chance to learn as much as you can about Sweden. It may sound too optimistic, but it works!

How else can you make it easier for yourself? The first and most important piece of advice has to be to learn the language. Any words you can learn before you move will help you a great deal. The second is to make some friends. Other immigrants are often the easiest to befriend and most supportive, simply because they will share your complains and won't be hurt by your comments as the Swedes would. By all means make some Swedish friends as well – but remember they are a reserved people, so don't feel hurt or discouraged if it takes you longer than expected. Finally, get busy! If you don't work, join local sports, crafts, or educational groups. Lead a language course, play football with a local club. Sweden is the place to do it, Swedes love societies. The more involved you are the less you'll mind the differences, and you'll enjoy them instead.

The main key to surviving culture shock is preparation and understanding. Books like this one, and those listed in the back of the book, are there to help you. Remember to use Swedes as a resource – and make the most of your time in Sweden!

DO'S AND DON'TS
APPENDIX

DO

- Offer to take your shoes off or change to indoor shoes in private homes so that you don't track dirt, rain, or snow in. All Swedes do this.

- Bring flowers, wine or chocolates with you when you visit a Swedish home for a meal or an evening. Don't forget to take the paper or the plastic from the flowers before you present them to your hostess.

- Remember to thank your hostess or host for the meal while still at the table, and to say *tack för senast* – 'thanks for last' – when you next see her or him.

- Take a number at the chemist, post office, *Systembolaget* or any other shop or office where you need to queue. Without one you won't be served.

DON'T

- Be late to a social engagement, work commitment or any appointment. Five minutes is considered rude; over fifteen is unforgivable if you don't know the person you're meeting well.

- Criticise Sweden, even to people you are friendly with. There is an unwritten international rule that anyone is welcome to criticise their own country, but no foreigner should ever join in, particularly if they are living in the country themselves! You may not think the Swedes you are with mind, but they do.

- Worry about tipping – the price is generally inclusive. However, many people will round the bill up in a taxi or at an evening meal in a restaurant.

CULTURAL QUIZ

Now that you have some inside knowledge of the way Swedish society operates, you can test yourelf with the following questions. As with any culture there are not always definitive responses to every situation but the Swedish character is such that in most cases the best response should be fairly obvious to you.

After the initial settling in period and as you begin to feel as though you fit into your new surroundings, the benefits and drawbacks of living and staying in Sweden will become a part of your own lifestyle. When you have reached this point, congratulations – now you are a real Svensson!

SITUATION ONE

You have been invited to a Swedish colleague's home for dinner at 7:30 p.m. You are looking forward to seeing their home and eating Swedish food, and have bought some wine to take with you. They live on the other side of town, and there are only two buses an hour to their area. One would get you there at 7:45 p.m. and the other at 7:15 p.m. Do you:

    A   Decide you'll drive; you don't plan to get drunk anyway.

    B   Take the later bus; there's nothing worse than being early to someone's house, and you've always heard that twenty minutes late is simply fashionable.

    C   Take the earlier bus, even though it's a nuisance.

Comments

You could drive, but then you won't be able to drink at all. It's not a question of not getting drunk in Sweden. The drink driving laws are so strict that you'll need to refuse the wine you're taking with you. However, if you do drive, your hosts will certainly understand and respect that you cannot drink that evening.

Taking the late bus is the only 'wrong' option – it will mean that you arrive later than the stated 7:30 p.m. time. This is the time that your host and hostess are expecting you to arrive at their house, and they will have timed their cooking of the meal and the rest of the evening accordingly. Punctuality is expected and arriving late is generally considered impolite.

If other guests are invited and you are late they will all be waiting for you, probably uncomfortably. A cocktail hour is not common in Sweden. The best option is to take the early bus and you can arrive at their door at 7:30 p.m. exactly. If you're five or ten minutes early that's fine, Swedes will be used to it.

SITUATION TWO

You and your child are taking the bus, or the tram or subway. He is complaining and wants some chocolate from one of the kiosks, but you don't want him to spoil his dinner. He starts to work himself up into a state and screams and, in the crowded area, you are not sure what to do. Do you:

A Start to scream back at him to stop him.

B Give him a sharp slap and tell him he'll be in trouble when you get home.

C Ask him calmly not to scream. If necessary, get off the bus until he stops, or cuddle him.

D Warn him he'll be punished by his other parent when you get home.

Comments

Every culture has different ways of raising children and just because you have moved to Sweden does not mean you need to adopt all of their ideas about children. However, you should be aware that option B is illegal wherever you are in Sweden, and therefore cannot be recommended!

You may not threaten or physically harm a child in public or at home. If you try to intimidate your child with promises of punishment at home you will probably violate this law as well. Swedes prefer not to intervene in family matters, but if they think you are harming your child they may well.

Screaming back is ineffective, but may make you feel better. Unfortunately you will also incur the disapproval of all around you if you do so (not least because of the increased noise). The Swedish option would be C – frustrating at times but moderate.

SITUATION THREE

You are working in a company that needs an overhaul of its ordering system. Part of your job is to work out which system would be most effective. You settle down to work on this and, at around 4:00 p.m. one afternoon, you have come up with a solution. It's such a good solution that you feel it needs to be implemented immediately. Do you:

A   Call an immediate meeting of all staff and explain the new system to them.

B   Send a memorandum around to everyone, telling them about the new system.

C   Send a memorandum around to everyone, asking them to come to a meeting the next day to talk about ways of implementing the new system.

Comments

Option B is the most efficient, which would seem Swedish, but in fact it would come across as impersonal, and worse, imperious. The idea of consensus is very important to Swedes in business as well as everyday life, and your colleagues will expect to be involved in the decision. (This is becoming more and more true in everyday business life in many other countries also.)

The same lack of consultation is a problem with Option A, but a bigger problem is going to be that many people in Sweden work from 8–4, and they will not want to stay back for an unplanned meeting. Swedish workers are industrious, and won't in general refuse to work overtime, but they value their free time and won't want to work over if it isn't absolutely necessary.

Option C is the best, but make sure that when you present your solution at the meeting you are ready for discussion of the system before it is adopted through consensus.

SITUATION FOUR

You are at a party where you know only a few of the guests. Most of the others seem to know each other, and you feel uneasy as you cannot keep up with their Swedish. Do you:

A Wait for your host to introduce you to some of the other guests.

B Go up to the other guests and introduce yourself, asking in English what their name is and what they do.

C Turn to another guest and try to start a conversation in Swedish, asking also if they speak English.

D Find your host and ask if he will introduce you to some guests who speak English. You think, although you don't say this, that introducing you to people you can speak with is one of his duties as host.

Comments

Swedes prefer to introduce themselves, usually through shaking your hand and saying their names at the same time. You should give your name back while still shaking their hand. When you arrive, introduce yourself to the guests already there, rather than them making the effort to introduce themselves to you (another reason to arrive early at a party). Therefore options A and D are not the best ones.

Option B is good, but don't ask new acquaintances what they do at a party. Business and pleasure are kept separate and it is not common to identify yourself through your work to the same extent as it is in other countries. Having to speak English may make some Swedes nervous or uncomfortable, so you may have to try this option with several different people.

Option C is probably the best one. Many people approached this way will switch to English after you have tried in Swedish. If you introduce yourself before starting the conversation you will fit in best.

SITUATION FIVE

You are taking your child to her new childcare centre. She will be at the centre every day after school until you pick her up after work, and you want her to feel comfortable there. When you arrive, you see the children playing out in the snow. You go into the centre and are met by a young man, who seems to be one of main carers. You are a little surprised by both of these things. Do you:

A Ask the young man if you can speak to one of the carers. He must be an administrative worker, and you can explain what the carer needs to know directly to her. You are sure that he is not interested in hearing the details – after all, men aren't usually interested in the details of looking after children.

B Start to discuss the details of your child's care with the young man. You want to know how long the children will be playing outside, and if they go outside even when it is actually snowing, and if your child can stay inside on such days as she's not used to such cold weather.

C Settle down to discuss the schedule and details with the young man. You are impressed by his professionalism and rapport with your child already, and ask if you should pack a change of clothing with your child everyday, in case she gets wet from playing in the snow.

D Say you don't want a man looking after your child – it's unnatural – and you don't want her playing outside all the time when there is a perfectly good inside area for her to play and learn in. If the young man can't promise a female carer and inside educational play you'll take your child elsewhere.

Comments

Option D is clearly extreme. Men and women do share childcare in Sweden, and it's considered a plus for children to have male carers, rather than unnatural. The majority of childcarers are still women, so there will always be a mix at whatever childcare centre you choose. Another problem with Option D is that you may not be able to take your child elsewhere – childcare places are not unlimited, and you may have to put her on a waiting list.

Option C is the best option – you should prepare yourself for the Swedish way of childcare so that you aren't really surprised by the differences.

Options A and B show that you are not used to the idea of male childcarers or outdoor play and education. Children learn through play, whether indoors with educational toys or outdoors in the snow or sunshine. Neither option is particularly offensive to Swedes, who will often accept that you are probably ignorant (after all, you're a foreigner, you'll be forgiven!). The carer in these cases is likely to explain how it works in the childcare centre, and that you have no need to worry. Give it a try before you threaten anything – threats are not taken lightly in Sweden.

SITUATION SIX

You have a good working relationship with your colleagues, and have settled into the Swedish office from the overseas headquarters well. However, you don't feel you know many of your colleagues socially, and after three weeks you'd like to meet some more of them. In the canteen one day you sit down with an acquaintance and start a conversation. Which topic do you pick?

A Ask your acquaintance about work – How's it going in their area? What exactly do they do? Is it very busy? and so on.

B Comment that it's been very grey and cold lately. Does it ever get better than this? You feel quite depressed by the weather and miss the sunshine of home. When does the summer begin?

C Mention your family and ask about your acquaintance's. Is he married? Does he have children? What are their ages?

D Ask for her opinion about the current political situation. Can she explain the different sides to you? Which party does she think is right?

Comments

Keep in mind from the beginning that Swedes are reserved and you run the risk of alarming anyone that you approach like this. However, Swedes are generally friendly and willing to make friends – if slowly.

Option A could work, although it may seem a bit like an inquisition. In general, Swedes prefer not to discuss work in their free time but as a starting topic it is not bad.

The weather is a favourite topic in Sweden, so Option B is a good one. Although you should not criticise Sweden in general, criticising the weather is acceptable – Swedes do it themselves all the time. But don't overdo comments about how much better it is in your country.

Option C could be perceived as a bit nosy. Swedes keep themselves to themselves until they know you better. If you want to volunteer information about your family, fine, but don't pry into theirs until you know them better.

Finally, Option D could be an excellent conversation starter, especially if you ask to have a specifically Swedish situation explained to you. It's not unusual to discuss politics in Sweden, but it is not usual to ask which party a Swede supports. Unlike other countries, where you can discover who a person supports through his conversation, in Sweden a political conversation will often be a general discussion of pros and cons.

Another safe topic would have been sport, particularly if Swedish teams or athletes are doing well in international competition, or new films or television. The rules governing polite conversation are the same in Sweden as elsewhere, with the proviso that Swedes are more cautious about opening up, and that you should respect their reserve.

CALENDAR OF FESTIVALS
AND HOLIDAYS

Public holidays in Sweden are sometimes called 'Sundays' to confirm that they are not ordinary working days.

13th December	St Lucia Day (Not a public holiday but the beginning of the Christmas season)
24th December	Christmas Eve (*julafton*) (When Swedes celebrate Christmas)
25th December	Christmas Day (A public holiday)
26th December	*Annandag Jul* (like British Boxing Day) (A public holiday)
1st January	New Year's Day (A public holiday)
6th January	Epiphany (A public holiday)
13th January	*Trettondag Knut* (Not a public holiday but the day Swedes take down their Christmas decorations)
February	winter school holidays – referred to as *Sport Lov* as many take the opportunity to go skiing
February/March	Shrove Tuesday (The last Tuesday before Lent, when Swedes eat special cakes called semlor)
March/April	Good Friday, Easter Sunday and Easter Monday (As Friday and Monday are public holidays, many schools take a week off.)

25th March	Waffle Day
	(Our Lady Day, when Swedes eat waffles.)
30th April	Walpurgis Night
	(not a public holiday)
1st May	International Labour Day
	(a public holiday with many parades)
May	Ascension Day
	(a public holiday – a Thursday six weeks after Easter)
May/June	Whitsunday and Whitmonday
	(both public holidays, about 10 days after Ascension Day)
6th June	Swedish Flag Day
	(not a public holiday)
3rd week of June	Schools break up for the summer
24th June	Midsummer Day
	(this is a public holiday, but is in fact most celebrated on Midsummer's Eve, which is the Friday closest to the 24th June.)
July	Many Swedes take 3 or 4 weeks' holiday in a row in July
August	time to celebrate crayfish coming in season, with crayfish parties
1st November	All Saints Day
	(a public holiday)
10th November	St Martin's Day
	(not a public holiday, but a day to eat goose which are now at their best.)
End November	1st Sunday in Advent
	(four Sundays before Christmas, and time to start thinking about celebrating again)

GLOSSARY

Ja	yes
nej	no
hej	hello
goddag	good day
god morgon	good morning
god kväll	good evening
god natt	good night
hur mår du?	how are you?
bara bra, tack	fine, thank you
det var trevligt att träffas	it was nice to meet you
hejdå	good bye
tack	thank you
tack så mycket; tusen tack	thank you so much
varsågod	you're welcome or do go ahead (such as when holding a door, or waiting) to start eating
ingen fara	no problem
snälla	please (this is not a direct translation but one can use this to mean please)
förlåt, förlåt mig	sorry, forgive me
ursäkta, ursäkta	excuse me
går det bra om ...	is it all right if ... (literal translation is 'goes it well if..')
pratar du engelska?	
talar du engelska?	do you speak English?
hjälp	help
vi ses; vi hors	see you soon; speak soon (on the phone)

194

RESOURCE GUIDE

Most official websites in Sweden offer at least some information in English. Look for a Union Jack flag, or a mention of 'Other Languages' if you don't see a link straight to English. Some of the links are not immediately obvious!

EMERGENCIES

The emergency numbers are **112** or **90000** (the former is an EU agreed number). Use these numbers if you need an ambulance, the police or the fire department.

For a medical emergency you can also phone your local emergency care centre (the number will be in the blue pages of the telephone directory), or go directly to your nearest hospital's casualty/accident and emergency departments.

HEALTH

When you have found a place to live, find the nearest local doctor to register with. For a detailed explanation of the system see **www.parentnetsweden.com** (click on 'Resources' and then 'Health').

HOUSING

Most of the major real estate agents are available online. For a list of current ones, see the website **www.americaninsweden.com** and look through the links. You can also find them listed on **www.gulasidorna.se.** Many Swedes rent, and you can rent for a contract of 3 months, 6 months or longer.

LANGUAGE

Your first call should be to the SFI centres (see page 85). You may also find information at the Education website on **www.skolverket.se**.

There are various online options for learning, such as *www.hhs.se/isa/swedish*; and there are also many online dictionaries (including one on the skolvertet website).

RELIGION

To find out more information about the Swedish Church, look at **www.svenskakyrkan.se**
If you need information about local places of worship in your areas, ask for the Religionsguide from the Immigration office, or again look at the local yellow pages.

GENERAL WEBSITES OF INTEREST
About Sweden

Tourist information   **www.gosweden.org**
All about Sweden   **www.virtualsweden.net**
The Swedish Institute   **www.si.se**
    Lots of information in English, with good links for both items of cultural interest and for students
Study in Sweden   **www.studyinsweden.se**

For expatriates

For Americans/Gothenburgers   **www.amerikanska.com**
    Lots of useful forums and people to give advice
For parents   **www.parentnetsweden.com**
    Lots of information and links to useful websites, including information on education, childcare, and other topics particularly of interest to parents.

Official websites

Swedish statistics   **www.scb.se/eng**
The parliamentary website   **www.riksdagen.se/english**
    Information about your local MP, and also about new laws.

Immigration service   **www.migrationsverket.se**

Downloadable applications, and clear explanations of immigration regulations

Swedish National Tax Board   **www.rsv.se**

Downloadable tax guide

Social Security Office   **www.fk.se**

Lots of information about what benefits you're entitled to, but in either Swedish or simplified Swedish

FURTHER READING

This is a combination of the books I used myself and the books you may like to read either before or when you have moved to Sweden. They will probably help you with the transition, or at the very least kindle some excitement in you at the thought of your move!

However, it's not easy to find books about Sweden abroad, and you may have better luck with books about Scandinavia in general. Swedish firms do publish some books in English, but these can be expensive – you can find them in any good Swedish library though.

The Swedish Institute publishes many fact sheets on different topics. You can order these by post from the Swedish Institute, PO Box 7434, 103 91, Stockholm, Sweden. I have also given suggestions on Swedish literature, language books and cookery books below.

Useful Books for the Traveller

Blue Guide to Sweden, Mary Alderton, A & C Black, 1995. A tourist guide specialising in the historical and artistic elements of the country. Dry at times but enjoyable.

The Rough Guide to Scandinavia, Jules Brown and Mick Sinclair, The Rough Guides, 1993. Also covers Norway, Finland and Denmark, and has an extensive section on the history of each country, as well as what to see and where to go. An updated *Scandinavia* guide is due out in 1997, along with another guide specifically for Sweden. *The Rough Guide to Sweden* will have more information on the culture and history of Sweden itself (due spring 1997).

Scandinavian & Baltic Europe, Greg Videon and others, Lonely Planet Publications, 1993. Sweden, Norway, Finland, Denmark, Iceland and all three Baltic nations are included. The Sweden section gives a useful overview on what to see and where to go.

Baedeker's Scandinavia, Jarrold & Sons Ltd. Covering Sweden, Norway, Denmark and Finland from a motoring tourist's perspective. Good if you plan to travel within Scandinavia on holiday.

In addition, other guides, such as the *Insight Guide to Sweden, Fodor's Guide to Sweden* and others, offer useful advice on travelling in Sweden. The *Insight Guide* includes essays on Swedish customs, history and everyday life, intended for the traveller but useful also for the long term visitor.

Swedish for Travellers, Lausanne, Switzerland: Berlitz Guides, 1989. Gives commonly used Swedish phrases, plus advice on ordering in restaurants.

Useful Books for Immigrants

Living and Working in Sweden, Monica Rabe, Tre Böcker Förlag, 1994. Looks at life in Sweden from the perspective of a Swede who has lived abroad.

Live & Work in Scandinavia, Victoria Pybus and Susan Dunne, Vacation Work, 1994. Includes detailed information on moving to and living in Sweden, Denmark, Finland, Iceland and Norway, including many addresses. Much of the information is specific to British emigrants, but useful for others as well.

Amusing Reading

Xenophobe's Guide to the Swedes, Peter Berlin, Ravette Books, 1994. A pocket sized look at the foibles of the 'average' Swede.

Visst är det Härligt att vara Svensk! Rikard Fuchs, Wahlström & Widstrand, 1991. For when you have learned Swedish – a Swede pokes fun at the stereotypical Swede. (The title means 'Of course it's wonderful to be Swedish!')

Available from the Government/Local Authorities

Sports in Sweden, Swedish Sports Confederation, Arvidsson and Yrlid (Information Sweden), 1994.

Sweden - a general introduction for immigrants, Swedish Immigration Board, AB Fälths Tryckeri, 1986.

Nature in Sweden, P Hanneberg, Swedish Institute.

Swedish Forest, Skogsstyrelsen (National Board of Forestry).

History and Politics

The Vikings, Johannes Brondsted, Penguin, 1983.

The Vikings, Else Roesdahl, Penguin.

Runes in Sweden, Sven Jansson, 1987.

The Gods and Myths of Northern Europe, Penguin.

Gustavus Adolphus: A History of Sweden 1611-1632, M Roberts.

The Swedish Imperial Experience 1560-1718, Michael Roberts, Cambridge 1984.

A Concise History of Sweden, A Åberg, 1987.

Sweden: The Nation's History, Franklin D. Scott, 1988.

Swedish Politics During the 20th Century, S Hadenius.

A Crisis of the Welfare State?, Axel Hadenius, Coronet, 1987.

Committed Neutral: Swedish Foreign Policy, Cranford Sundelius, editor, 1989. With essays on Sweden's policy of neutrality.

Festivities and Food

Majstång, Kräftor och Lucia – Svenska festseder, Jan-Öjvind Swahn, The Swedish Institute, 1994. A lovely treasury of Swedish customs and holidays. Also available in English (under the name of

Maypoles, Crayfish and Lucia – Swedish Holidays and Traditions), French and German.

Traditional Handicraft from Sweden, Svenska Hemslödsföreningen.

The Swedish Kitchen – A Culinary Journey, Lennart Hagerfors and the Swedish Culinary Team, Norstedts Förlag, 1995. Includes 198 recipes from south to north featuring modern Swedish food, with commentary on their origins.

A Small Treasury of Swedish Food, Federation of Swedish Farmers.

Swedish Cooking, ICA Förlaget, 1983.

Pâterisserie of Scandinavia, J Audrey Ellison, Macdonald Orbis, 1989.

Design and Art

A History of Swedish Art, Lyberg Lindgren and Wahlberg Sandström, 1987.

Nordic Folk Art, M Nodermann.

Manor Houses and Royal Castles in Sweden, B Söderberg.

Quality Made in Sweden, Gunnar Hedin, Informationsförlaget.

Literature

An Anthology of Modern Swedish Literature, Merrick, 1989.

The four *Emigrants* books, by Vilhem Moberg, which tell the tale of a Swedish family's emigration to America in the 19th century.

Both modern and traditional literature by Swedish authors will give you a taste of Sweden – among the best who have been translated into English are August Strindberg, Stig Dagerman, Kerstin Ekman, Selma Lagerlöf, Sara Lidman, Agneta Pleijel, Bent Söderberg and Hjalmar Söderberg.

Reading for Children

The Pippi Longstocking and the Emil books, all by Astrid Lindgren.

The Wonderful Adventures of Nils and *Further Adventures of Nils*, Selma Lagerlöf.

We Live In Sweden, Stephan Keeler and Chris Fairclough, 1984. A basic look at living in Sweden.

Business

Management and Society in Sweden, P Lawrence and T Spybey.

The Swedish Economy, Barry P Bosworth, Brookings 1987. Includes essays on all aspects of Sweden's economy, including the financing of its welfare state.

If you are connected to the World Wide Web, there are many excellent sites from Sweden which offer information about specific topics. Swedes have embraced the idea of the Internet, and it's one of the European countries with the highest percentage of users. Most Swedish Internet sites are in both Swedish and English. The country code for Sweden is **.se**.

ABOUT THE AUTHOR

Charlotte Rosen Svensson grew up between cultures, with a Welsh mother and an English father, and emigrated to the United States with her family when she was a child. She went to school and college in the United States, Germany and Scotland, and decided to travel in Australasia after graduation. Settling in has always proved easier than travelling, however, and the year's trip turned into living and working in Sydney and living briefly in Hong Kong, with some backpacking in between.

After two months in India and three months in the US, she moved to London to work in publishing. After London came Sweden in order to live with a Swede met in Bangkok, and work as a language teacher. After Sweden she took up a position in Oxford, working in international promotions for African and Caribbean authors.

Throughout life she hopes to continue travelling and above all learning about different cultures and people.

INDEX